How To Climb Mount Everest in Sandals

The courage to live an ordinary life

RHIANNON REES

How To Climb Mount Everest in Sandals

*The courage
to live an
ordinary life*

Copyright © Rhiannon Rees 2011
Address: PO Box 1698, Kingscliff NSW 2487
Email: *yourlife@lovelivingthedream.com*

Cover Image: Alana Couch Photography © 2011
Author's Image: Lyn Taylor Photography © 2011

Editor: Alex Mitchell *www.authorsupportservices.com*
Sub Editor: Tracey Wiltshire *www.boundwithheart.com.au*

First published in Australia 2011 by The Publishing Queen
Copyright © 2011 *www.thepublishingqueen.com*

ISBN 978-1-921673-35-1

About The Author

RHIANNON REES
B.Bus, D.C.H, H.M.C, R.C.S.Hom

Business Coach
Ranked 4th Best Business Coach in the World 2010
www.ActionCOACH.com/rhiannonrees

Humanitarian, homeopath, entrepreneur, writer, presenter, mother of one, lover of life and now with this book, Rhiannon is a first time author.

Rhiannon makes regular appearances on television and radio, and writes for a number of newspapers.

Rhiannon's mission is to assist and empower people to live full lives of happiness, meaning, fun and passion.

www.LoveLivingTheDream.com

Dedication

For the light of my life, my son Jaiesh
Without the unconditional love we share
and the joy I feel when you are in my arms,
I may never have found the reason
to change our lives.

I love you to the moon and back.

- Your Mama -

Family Tree of Rhiannon Rees

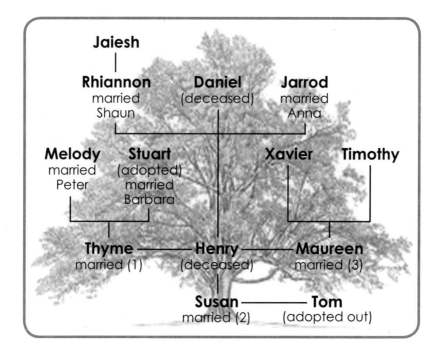

Jaiesh

Rhiannon
married
Shaun

Daniel
(deceased)

Jarrod
married
Anna

Melody
married
Peter

Stuart
(adopted)
married
Barbara

Xavier

Timothy

Thyme ———— **Henry** ———— **Maureen**
married (1) (deceased) married (3)

Susan ———— **Tom**
married (2) (adopted out)

Acknowledgements

I would like to thank everyone that I have shared my life experiences with – you have taught me so much and it has been such a rich journey. There are so many people to thank; if you are not mentioned here, just know that I really do appreciate and acknowledge all that you have done for me.

My son has been my greatest gift of love, and for that I am eternally grateful. I am so glad to have such a wonderful friendship with my mum. Without the dedication and hard work that my mother put into this labour of love, you would not be reading this right now. I would also like to thank Melanie, for offering me so much stability when I was a child. To my brothers, I have always loved you.

Thank you to my dearest and sweetest childhood friend, the most beautiful Sunny Gilbert. Thank you so much to Marie Cochrane who is such a guiding light in my life. Thank you to my friends, Paula Gleeson, Amanda Patterson, Marilla and Shaun, for their constant support. Thank you to Suzie Q (Taylor) for your amazing dedication to our workshops and retreats, without which they would not be the high quality that they are.

Thank you to Rose Marcus for her ongoing support and also to Adele Anderson and Pennie and Hal Garvie. Without your help I may not have been able to return to Australia to look after my mum – your generosity astounds me.

Thank you to Brad Sugars and the team. Working in the world of business coaching has been the beginning of a journey of abundance and revelation of what I am truly capable of.

Thank you to Kylee, The Publishing Queen, who held my hand every step of the way and to whom I owe so much. To Alex Mitchell and Tracey Wiltshire for their magic in weaving the story together, as well as their incredible dedication and long hours of hard work to bring this to fruition, I am eternally grateful.

Thank you to Deanna Papineau, Victoria Downes, Janice and Larry Carr, Ali McLean, and Jo Younker, Jill Dorken and Donnie Blunden for your wonderful friendship over the years. Thank you also to Justine McKell, Eloise King and Gillian Anderson who graciously offered their testimonials. And many thanks to Sue Kennedy.

I would like to acknowledge those people who have been significantly influential in my life: Michelle Everett-Morgan, Dalai Lama, Mother Teresa, Murray Feldman, Lou Klein, and all the Indian homeopaths.

Most of all, I want to thank my great therapists and advisors who unlocked my door to freedom, and showed me my very own key to happiness.

Thank you. *Namaste*

Introduction

"Always say 'yes' to the present moment.
It is so futile to create inner resistance to what already is.
What could be more insane than to oppose life itself,
which is now and always 'now'?
Surrender to what is.
Say 'yes' to life and see how life suddenly starts
working for you rather than against you."

Eckhart Tolle

I spent years in analysis, immersing myself in self knowledge, to advance myself spiritually and gain insight into getting the most out of life. But it seemed that all the books I read focussed on achieving the peaks, getting to the top of the mountain ahead of everyone else. No-one talked about just *being*. What about the simple satisfaction of being born, going to school, having a job, getting married, having kids and growing old? Being happy and content just living an ordinary life? Perhaps achieving these seemingly small goals was not as ordinary as I had first thought. Perhaps what I had thought was ordinary, was actually extraordinary.

I lost my innocence through child sexual abuse, lost contact with my mother for most of my childhood, lost my brother to suicide, lost five babies to miscarriage, lost all my money, lost my husband to his other identity as a woman, and even lost the roof over my head and became homeless. Each of these losses carved into my soul, and I thought I would never survive.

But I did.

Going to the core of myself allowed me the freedom

to understand what was truly important. That all there is worth living for is love. I learned to love unconditionally and to forgive. I learned that if you hold a loving space for yourself this will emanate to everyone else, and I learned that you can have some fun doing it. I learned to treasure the small moments that make life special.

I wasn't ready to learn all this until I had lost everything; but it doesn't have to be that hard. It's really only a matter of understanding what is truly important, and where the gems lie. The control we have over our mind is all we truly ever have. It is an extraordinary and powerful gift. We all can access and use this great power inside ourselves. *How To Climb Mount Everest in Sandals* will help you discover and spark your fire inside.

It is my destiny and my great joy to help others. If I can change the life of one person, then through this, many lives will change. If I can shed some light on your journey and help you to see that your dawn is almost breaking and that your day will be truly beautiful, then I have done my job.

Contents

- Chapter One -
A Wonderful Start

"Through our great good fortune, in our youth our hearts were touched with fire. It was given to us to learn at the outset that life is a profound and passionate thing."

Oliver Wendell Holmes

The first eight years of my life were very smooth. I don't have any bad memories of this time.

My brother Daniel and I were very close and were often left to look after each other. Daniel was two years older than me, and Mum said we stuck together like glue. She could never figure out who did what as we would never give each other away and let the team down. So, whenever we were in trouble, she simply punished both of us together.

Daniel was rather timid; Mum said he was 'born sad'. I stuck up for him at school. If we got into trouble, I would take the lead and then look back at Daniel and ask for acknowledgement with, 'Daniel, isn't that so?' to which he would simply nod shyly. He helped me out as well, like the time I wet my pants on the way to preschool and Daniel gave me his to wear.

Our favourite place to be together was a big hole in the backyard. The two of us would often go out and sit in it. I love the feeling of finding a perfect place and just sitting quietly. If we were really good, our parents would bring home a bag of sugared almonds. Oh how we loved those! I still think of sugared almonds as a reward for being a good girl.

My dad was a fabulous doctor and a crazy scientist, all rolled up into one eccentric package. He was a brilliant doctor and people travelled from far and wide to see him, but he always had some hare-brained crazy scheme on the go, like importing pink champagne from Russia, or building a chocolate factory in China when it was still a totalitarian regime. Once he decided to purchase lanterns from a small town along the Murray River, and then sell them on to suppliers all over the country. Another idea was to breed Charolais cattle, so he started Colo Charolais Stud. Of course, as Dad worked full time as a doctor, Mum was left to run the cattle stud, even though she hardly knew the back end of the bull from the front. If my dad had not been so pigheaded and eccentric, they may have stayed together, who knows.

I think they were both stubborn and they created a catastrophe together, neither one of them having any parents to talk to. My father's parents and his sister were all killed in a car accident when my father was about thirty, and Mum was estranged from her father, her mother having deserted her many years earlier.

All Mum wanted was to stay at home and raise her three children, but she ended up travelling the world, to New Zealand, Europe and the United States, bringing back champion livestock and sperm for the cattle stud. She was away from her children for a week or two at a time every couple of months, but did become a very successful breeder. Mum was one of the first farmers in Australia to use IVF in breeding, and her cows and bulls were winners at the Royal Shows. She won 'Supreme Animal' for this and 'Champion' for that. Of course, Mum did it all with her own style, and always in designer clothes. One of her more memorable public relations campaigns involved literally having a bull in a china shop. It was behind a tiny rope fence and created quite a spectacle. Mum always said those big bulls were so placid, like little kittens really.

From around six years of age, I had the responsibility of tending Mum's precious vegetable garden while she was on her overseas trips. I took my responsibility very seriously even at that age, and would pull up the carrots, onions and radishes to see how they were growing. This probably thwarted their growth a teensy bit, but how could I tend a garden if I couldn't see the vegetables? Mum thought it was hilarious when I showed her how I looked after those vegetables so carefully.

Once, during a dinner party, Daniel and I declared loudly to the guests, 'Mum killed all our pets'. You can imagine the looks the guests gave Mum. It was priceless. Like many mums, our mum ended up feeding and looking after all our pets. We had a collection of jam jars and other containers on the windowsill in the kitchen, with holes in their lids. These were the homes we made for the spiders, cockroaches, small lizards and other bugs we collected from the garden. Mum used fly spray to kill a handful of flies, which she then distributed among the jars to feed the pets. The next day of course everything was dead.

Mum would sometimes go to Paddy's Markets and bring home live crabs to prepare for dinner. Sometimes we would take off the rubber bands from around their claws and watch them scamper across the floor, away from the big pot of bubbling water. No matter how fast they ran, they always ended up as dinner.

My parents moved to Millicent in South Australia in 1972, the year before I began primary school. We had so much fun on the long drive there; Daniel and I had beautiful colouring books and pencils to keep us busy. Living on the farm was idyllic. It began a love in me for wide open spaces, nature and farm animals. It seemed in the five years that we were there I never got to see the entire property.

In second grade, I started to try out various sports, as most children do. Ballet was the first – I wore a green tutu and as I didn't have ballet tights, I covered my legs in Mum's expensive Guerlain foundation. With one bottle spread over each leg, it looked just like ballet tights! Eventually, I chose netball, which was lucky, as it turned out I was going to be six foot tall, but I also enjoyed running, swimming and horse riding. Later on, I became so grateful for my sports. They gave me a place where I didn't have to think about my home life.

When I was eight, my parents had their third child

together, little Jarrod. Eight months later, Mum left the family. All she wanted was to be a stay-at-home mother, but she had been forced to become a business woman, travelling the world. Dad thought she would never leave the lifestyle or the money. He was wrong.

– Chapter Two –
A New Family Environment

"Wherever I look, I see signs of the commandment to honour one's parents and nowhere of a commandment that calls for the respect of a child."

Alice Miller

After the break-up of my parents, Daniel went to boarding school in Adelaide, and Jarrod and I were in foster care for a while. I always wanted a little sister, so I would call Jarrod 'Jane' and parade him around in the pram in the most colourful and girly little dresses.

One day, Dad came to see us, but they would not let him into the house as he had not booked an appointment. I could see my dad out of the window, holding up a gift he had bought me – a beautiful blue t-shirt with a picture of a cool surfer on it. I was not even allowed to go outside to give him a hug or receive my gift. I think it was around this time that Dad attempted suicide.

Before Mum left, Dad had been having an affair with the nurse at the local hospital. Eventually, that nurse became my stepmother and we went back to the farm to live with her and Dad, then moved to Sydney soon after.

She didn't want us three children, not her own, and let us know freely. She wore the pants in the household and had no hesitation in punishing us physically. I was regularly beaten, slapped and even had a plate broken over my head. One day, I accidentally walked in on my dad and stepmother in a very intimate situation and my stepmother took my hair and ripped it out of my head, she was so mad at me.

I soon learned to be a 'yes' girl. When my stepmother asked if I liked something, I asked her if she liked it before I answered. If she said 'yes', I said 'yes' also. If she said 'no', then I didn't like it either.

I began to lose my confidence and my ability to speak my mind, as the consequences of saying the wrong thing were dire. I would do anything not to rock the boat. I agreed with whatever everyone else said, and would even take the blame for things other people did. I didn't get my voice back until I was around twenty eight.

As soon as Mum left, it was made very clear that I was not allowed to see her, although I was only eight years old.

She did try to visit us, but was never let into our house, or was told we were on holidays. Once Mum came to the front door and I could hear her on the other side. Without opening the door, my stepmother said, 'Sorry, the children are not feeling well.' I urgently shoved my fingers under the door in the hope that Mum might see them and know that we were there. I heard her voice fading as she retreated from the front door, knowing that once again we wouldn't be able to see her.

One day, instead of going to violin lessons, I snuck out to see Mum. Soon, I started skipping violin lessons regularly to spend time with her.

When Dad found out about my secret visits to Mum, he said that if I did it again I would be put into foster care. I was so frightened that I did not see Mum again until I was eighteen.

Right then and there I developed a subconscious belief that would take years to uncover. I developed a belief that would be life changing. I began to believe that if I was happy, terrible things would happen and I would be excommunicated from my family. I lived with this belief for many years until I was fortunate enough to have Adlerian therapy as an adult. Because I believed it, this fear came true again and again through my life. From this one incident, I grew into an adult who believed that if I got involved with someone, they would either leave me or die. So I never risked that closeness again. I remained aloof in relationships and was always the one who broke it off. I had to protect myself from being hurt.

In Sydney, I went to a really nice private school, Kambala. I would pick up my younger brother from day care on my way home from school, and make dinner at night while my stepmother studied at Macquarie University. As I was only nine, it was pretty much the same food every night – lamb loin chops with mashed potatoes and peas.

In the end, I attended eight different primary schools and two high schools. I developed great skills in befriending people and making them feel special quite quickly, which was very useful down the track.

I was always the good kid at school, trying to keep everyone happy. As I got older, I became the class clown, hiding behind my humour so that nobody could see who I really was. There was no leeway at home and the punishment was pretty severe if I stepped out of line. I was afraid of my stepmother – I think half the town was. She ruled with an iron fist, while my dad looked on through the smoky haze of his constantly-lit cigarette.

Looking back now, I am more compassionate about my stepmother's situation. She was about twenty six when she married Dad, and he was nearly fifty. She inherited three children: an eight-month-old baby, an eight-year-old and an eleven-year-old. She was probably doing the best she could do in quite challenging circumstances, with three children to raise and a husband who worked long hours.

When I was eighteen, I was finally taller than my stepmother. One day, she was shouting at me about something, I think it was that I needed to get another part time job. Apparently, the three jobs I already had weren't enough. She was poking me in the chest to make her point. It was right on the breastbone where there is no flesh, so it was quite painful. On and on she went, until I started to feel myself rising up inside like a volcano. If she poked me in the chest one more time I was going to take her head off. I could see in my mind's eye my arm coming out from my side and up until it fairly and squarely took her head right off.

All the years of abuse, the constant bullying and feeling

that I was living my life in a cage had come to this point, and I had had enough. The rage welled up inside me. Just as my stepmother was about to poke me again, she looked up into my eyes and saw the change. She pulled her finger away at the last minute, and never hit me again.

After this, I decided to get back in touch with my mother. Even at eighteen, the punishment was the same. I was excommunicated from the clan. I was never again allowed to come home, not even for a birthday or Christmas, and was forbidden from having a relationship with my brothers.

I remember my stepmother saying to me, 'I no longer take on the role of your mother. I will now step down.' Dad begged me to apologise to my step mum for finding my mother. I responded that I would not apologise for something that was not wrong.

Why should a child have to choose between their natural mother and their stepmother? There should be enough love to have both in their lives. Love is love, it knows no boundaries. It is so sad that my stepmother went to such great lengths to tear our family apart, but I guess without these experiences I would not be who I am today, so for that I am grateful.

Being separated from my mother from such a young age, and then later from the rest of my family, has affected me in so many ways. Even now, my mum comes over to babysit and encourages me to go out and enjoy myself, but all I want to do is to be home, spending time with my family. No matter how hard I try, I can never make up for all that lost time, all those years I pined for us to be together. This was one of Daniel's wishes – that the family would 'one day' be together again. When you are a kid, you don't really know what 'one day' means.

- Chapter Three -
A Predator Stalks

*"You may have trod me in the very dirt.
But still, like dust, I'll rise."*

Maya Angelou

For Christmas when I was ten, my father took the whole family to see *Star Wars*. He loved that movie; I think we saw it about eight times while it was showing at the cinema. Before the movie, there was a short film about the most picturesque and charming area of Australia called the Tweed Valley. My dad was mesmerised. He fell in love with it straightaway and by the next week we were all planning a holiday there.

We spent about a month in the area, staying at Mt Warning Lodge, where I remember catching a horse to ride. I was trying to be smart and ride him with only a halter. Of course, I fell off, right into a green ants' nest. Wow, do they sting! We hired a car, all of us packed in like sardines, and drove all around the area, occasionally stopping for tea or to ask for directions. It was a fabulous holiday.

About a month later, in early 1978, we moved there. We all lived in a one-bedroom house on the top of the hill at Uki. It was a one-horse town with a very hippy feel, but I liked it. I was still scared of my stepmother, but now I had other things to do. The Hare Krishna farm wasn't too far away, and I had a great time at Murwillumbah Primary School. I had to agree with my dad that this was a beautiful place.

We had a cute cocker spaniel called Bilbo, but somehow during the move he had either been left behind or lost. My parents arranged for someone to look after us for the weekend while they took Jarrod and went to look for Bilbo.

When I got home from school that day, I saw a box of magazines of naked children peeing and defecating. It belonged to the man who was minding us. Because I was only ten I didn't think about it much, but later on in the afternoon I walked past the bathroom door and noticed him having a shower with the door wide open. I thought this a little strange at the time, but was simply too young to know that something was wrong. So when we were going to bed I was shocked, scared and surprised when he forced himself upon my twelve-year-old brother and then me. He even bribed me with money and a gold chain if I would allow him to do more. All I could do was cry and pray that he would go away.

Finally in the wee hours of the morning he left the house. Daniel and I ran miles and miles down the road to our closest neighbours, and stayed there for the rest of the weekend. When Dad and my stepmother returned from Sydney we told them what had happened. I thought they would be so angry they would take a shotgun to him. However, it was never discussed again. I guess that's the only way they knew how to cope at that time. From then until I was about twenty, I would hyperventilate if I was with a man, and had a huge fear of being intimate.

- Chapter Four -
Memories Forever

"The most beautiful thing in life is that our souls remain over the places where we once enjoyed ourselves."
Kahlil Gibran

When I was eleven, we moved from that house to a family homestead with three bedrooms in Eungella. It was nice to have my own bedroom.

There was a beautiful curling river snaking through the property, and for the most part the road ran right beside the river. It would take us about half an hour to walk from our house to the gate to catch the bus to school, but we really enjoyed it. It was such a romantic looking property, undulating hills with mountains in the background and placid cows dotted all over the hillside, quietly eating grass.

I still think this is one of the prettiest pieces of land I have ever seen.

Bill, the owner of the property we were renting, was on crutches after suffering from polio as a kid, but he could drive his jeep with his hands and boy oh boy was he the boss. They had six kids and his wife had to manage just about everything.

My friends, Stacey and Sandra, were two of Bill's kids, and I would often go with them to find thunder eggs down by the swiftly rushing river. The sound of the water could be deafening as it crashed its way across massive boulders and channels. The thunder eggs were rocks packed full of crystals. I don't know how we knew which rocks held the glittering prize, but when smashed against another rock they would open up and shine with amazing iridescent colours.

Sometimes we would camp by the river and make damper. We wrapped it in foil and placed it in the hot coals of the fire we had built. It always tasted pretty disgusting no matter how we made it or how long we cooked it, but it was fun making it.

One day I brought a tortoise shell kitten home from Stacey and Sandra's house in my raincoat pocket. I loved Wargy, he would fall asleep around my neck at night, and Dad would come into my bedroom and put him outdoors. Once Dad had gone, I would sneak out and bring Wargy back in.

When I was eleven, we moved again, to another beautiful farm; this one a few minutes from Kingscliff, tucked in behind Cudgen in Northern NSW. My heart has been there ever since. This area of Australia is definitely my land, it's where I feel most relaxed. Just like a territorial animal, it is my country, my home, my walk and it's in my blood. It was also the place where I had one of the greatest loves of my life, my horse, Frank.

- Chapter Five -
A Girl's Best Friend

*"Three grand essentials to happiness in this life
are something to do, something to love
and something to hope for."*

Joseph Addison

I was eleven when my horse, Frank, came into my life, and I was barely without him until I was sixteen.

Frank was a big, strong, handsome bay thoroughbred, 16.2 hands tall. He came right off the track. The day we went to pick him up, someone else was riding him in the corral, trotting him around. I watched his neck flex perfectly, his fine legs flowing through the dust fluidly, moving his massive, strong frame effortlessly. He left a small trail of whimsical dust in his wake, as if nothing had passed by, not even a whisper.

As I watched the rider putting him through his paces, I thought, 'That's okay, you can ride him as long as you want, because when you are finished, I get to take him home forever.' In that moment we bonded. He was mine and I was his.

My childhood was very turbulent emotionally, and there was no love in our house. I felt unwanted and frightened a lot of the time. These distressing emotions were so vivid, overwhelming and constant, that the love and bond I shared with my horse were extremely comforting. I love horses. They are so regal and have such kind and sensitive hearts. Spending time with Frank, having something to care for, helped me enormously.

Frank was placid and gentle but could bolt like the wind. I rode him most days for hours at a time. Sometimes I would take him to the beach and my eyes would stream with salt and sweat as he tore up the sand at a lightning pace. He was just such a glorious animal.

I loved to sit in his feed box while he ate around me. He slobbered his feed all over me while I would talk to him. I even developed a liking for pony pellets – eating his food made me feel even closer to him. My whole life revolved around this horse. When I wasn't at school or sport, I was with Frank.

I took Frank to Pony Club most weekends and soon began to show him. We started with Gymkhanas and Jamborees and then went on to the Northern NSW show circuit: Woodenbong, Kyogle, Bangalow, Tweed Heads, Murwillumbah, Channon Dunnoon and Casino. Each weekend we went to a different competition.

In the flat riding competitions, points were given on the way you rode your horse, how subtle you were, how little you moved and the positioning of your body on the horse. I found these a little boring. The next round of competitions was about the horse, the way they moved their body, their shape and strength, their grooming and how they had been prepared for the show. The preparation process took hours, so my day would start at about 4 am, preparing my horse and my brother's horse.

In the afternoon were the sporting events and the jumping events, which were my favourite. I loved the feeling of a strong horse turning on a dime at a full gallop beneath you – it was truly exhilarating.

Frank would sometimes become a little nervous and skittish at the noise of the fairground rides at the shows. He would put on an act just like a child and instead of jumping over the obstacles, he would either go through them or around them.

It was a very full day, but I usually came away with a great feeling of accomplishment, a swag of different coloured ribbons, and anticipation for the next event.

As we drove away from competitions, we had streamers of brightly coloured ribbons hanging from our rear-view mirror. Anne Murray would be blasting on the stereo as we slowly meandered our way along the picturesque roads on our way home. The smell of horse, dust and manure lingered in the truck and to this day I simply adore this smell. To me it is the smell of happiness. If there was a perfume that smelt like this, I would wear it.

I had lots of trophies and literally garbage bags full of ribbons. Some of my girlfriends had their ribbons turned into bedspreads, or used them as vertical wallpaper in their bedrooms. Their rooms would spill over with brightly coloured stripes of satin and felt in red, blue, green, yellow and white.

There were plenty of girls in the riding competitions but fewer boys, so of course my brother won everything, without even practising! It was so annoying, I would spend hours training at home every day after school and my brother would simply get on his horse at any event and win.

Once, during a lunch break at an event, I tightened Frank's saddle to get ready for the next round of competition. I had Frank tied up to our horse trailer and there were other trailers around us. I did not realise that his saddle didn't fit him well, and was pressing on his withers, causing his back to ache. Tightening the saddle must have caused him a lot of pain, because he instantly moved backwards and forwards. He reared up and his legs went through the float next to him as he came down.

I was horrified as I saw my best friend in agony. I thought he must have broken his leg, which meant he would surely be put down. I heard a gasp escape from his mouth as though someone had just let the air out of a tyre; it was a horrible hissing sound. After his legs went through the float, he flipped over and began to choke on the rope that tied him to our float. The only love I had ever truly felt was from my best friend, my horse, Frank. I began to panic.

In a split second, people came from nowhere. Someone used a huge butcher's knife to slice the rope from his halter so that his head was free. Someone else jumped onto his belly and undid the saddle, throwing it off easily like you would throw a frisbee. All of a sudden, Frank looked so relieved and his bulging eyes relaxed. I was bawling as someone else gave me a new rope and Frank slowly and shakily got to his legs.

I don't think I breathed throughout the few minutes that the experience lasted. It seemed to last hours. Frank became even more precious to me once I saw the real possibility of losing him, and I became determined to spend even more time with him.

We got him a saddle that fitted him properly and had more room for his withers; it was a Keifer, German-made and absolutely divine. During the eight months it took Frank to recover, a chiropractor came out to our farm with a tennis ball and used it on Frank's back before picking up his legs and pulling them in all different directions. You could hear the pops and cracks as his legs went back into place. Eventually he made a full recovery, and I learned a lot about resilience and became stronger for it.

Frank was the greatest blessing in my childhood. I cherish all my memories with him. When I was sixteen I had to sell him to go to boarding school, which was incredibly stressful for me. I felt as if someone had sold my soul. It took years to overcome my grief.

He was sold to twin girls, Leanne and Jenny O'Reilly. I thought of him often, but could never bring myself to visit him. He was, after all, their horse now and I would most certainly want him back if I saw him. I did trust them to look after him as I knew them from Murwillumbah Pony Club and had competed against them in riding competitions.

Having Frank in my life taught me about the unfathomable depths of unconditional love. I learned how valuable it is to be able to care for something else. Giving selflessly to another, whether it is caring for another person, an animal or a plant, gives so much to the giver. Even in scientific terms, it has been shown that our serotonin levels go up when we are close to something we care for. For our mental and physical health, we really need something to love. There is much more to giving and contributing than we realise.

- Chapter Six -

Confinement

*"Children don't need much advice but they really
do need to be listened to and not just with half an ear."*

Emma Thompson

Grade ten was one of the best years of my life. I got the highest scores in the School Certificate for English and maths, as well as winning Best Athlete. I also won a couple of bikini beach girl competitions, 'Miss Redhead Matches' and 'Miss Eveready Batteries'. Try growing up being Miss Eveready! You can imagine the taunting – 'Ever ready for what?'

I found out later that I also won a scholarship to the Australian Institute of Sport as a heptathlete. My parents declined this offer without telling me I had won it. I was devastated when I found out, as the offer was no longer valid. Dad said he wanted me to go to university rather than waste my life on sport.

So Frank was sold and off I went for my senior years of high school to a private boarding school filled with toffee-nosed girls. The girls at the school seemed to be mainly concerned with trying to marry a rich farmer. I found it really hard to fit in, and this, along with grieving for my horse, meant my weight started to balloon. I put on about twenty kilos, going from a size ten to almost sixteen.

I was filling up on comfort food like pork loin chops dripping in oil, followed by mountains of ice cream. We had crazy competitions in the dining hall to see how many Weet-Bix we could eat with peanut butter and jam – I made the record one day by eating eighteen!

I didn't really notice my weight going up, and as I had been so skinny before it was easy to ignore. But I knew I had a problem. I just did not care about myself any more, since my horse had been sold.

I became depressed and reclusive, burying myself in study. I begged Dad over the phone to take me home. But he wouldn't and didn't. He had the opportunity to give me a great education, an opportunity he had never had as a child. In his mind, this was the best thing for me. But I was a pretty sensitive and affectionate kid, and I needed some encouragement. That 'tough love' thing didn't really work for me.

It was in year eleven when I had my first boyfriend. I didn't really know how to be close to someone, as I had continuously been separated from those I loved. Rather than risk the pain of being hurt, or learning how to overcome this pattern, I ended the relationship very quickly.

The belief systems we create as a child become the subconscious 'compass' for our lives. These beliefs are the ones that drive us toward a future which reflects these same beliefs, and so determine the decisions we make and ultimately the life we will lead.

- Chapter Seven -
Putting The Puzzle Together

"Kind words can be short and easy to speak.
But their echoes are truly endless."

Mother Teresa

The last thing Mum taught me to do before she left was how to shine my shoes. Like most eight–year-olds, I had no idea what leaving meant. It's hard at that age to understand the difference between someone leaving for a week, a fortnight, or the rest of your life. At that age you don't have enough wisdom or experience to understand what the concept of leaving really is.

I was very independent also, and can't say that I was shattered when she left. Although I missed her, it was more that I understood that my life had changed. The new environment, feeling caged, trapped and unloved by my stepmother and Dad, was so different to the way Mum had nurtured me.

After Mum left, Dad said negative things about her every day. According to him, Mum was bad, really bad. He also constantly commented, 'You are just like your mum'. Interestingly, when I did reconnect with my mum, to her credit she never told any stories, or said anything bad about Dad. I always respected her highly for that. She believed that firstly, he was my dad and secondly, bad tales could only reflect badly on the teller.

I didn't see Mum for around ten years. Although we children were forbidden to talk about her once she had gone, Dad constantly brought her up and kept her in his focus. I began to understand that Dad was still in love with Mum on some level. Hatred is one of the closest places that you can come to love and even as a child I knew that. He talked about her constantly, although everything he said was negative.

When I was about sixteen, I hopped off the school bus one day near Dad's work, to get a ride home with him. In the car, he began one of his tirades again about how terrible Mum was. I looked at him and said, 'You know Dad, if she was really that bad, you would never have married her'. Dad didn't respond, but in that moment I knew that I would not rest until I found my mum.

When I left school and started to look for a university, Dad wanted me to choose one close to home. He said that if I went to university in Brisbane, he would pay for my accommodation and buy me a car. But I was determined to go to Sydney, subconsciously wanting to look for Mum. Dad made it very clear that if I moved to Sydney, I was on my own. I knew that I needed to see Mum, although I didn't know the ramifications of that choice.

Once I moved to Sydney, I found the search for Mum to be pretty difficult. I had no luck with the Registry of Births, Deaths and Marriages, and so I began to contact her old boyfriends. This process alone took about a year. However, there was one boyfriend I couldn't track down, a Peter Cornelius.

One day, a relative of mine, who was a conductor with the Sydney Philharmonic Orchestra, was talking about the people in the orchestra and mentioned the Corneliuses, a husband and wife who both played in the group. Suddenly a light clicked for me. I asked him if he could find out if they were at all related to a Peter Cornelius.

He did ask them, and amazingly the man I was looking for was their son. I couldn't believe it! What an amazing stroke of luck to find him in this way, in a city of five million people and in an orchestra of only fifty. Peter Cornelius had a silent number, but my brother-in-law managed to get it for me. No wonder I had no luck finding him on my own! If this set of circumstances had not played out the way it did, I may never have found my mum.

I arranged to have coffee with Peter, and so many emotions went through me when he talked about Mum.

He had not seen her since she broke up with him and he didn't know where she was. Each word he said could have been the slimmest clue that would bring home the golden prize: finding my mum. The anticipation had me perched on the edge of my chair, practically toppling over as I leaned forward to listen to his every word. He smiled at me and said, 'You look so much like your mum. I have an idea. We used to use the same dry cleaner. Why don't you leave a message for her there?'

I thought there was no harm in trying, so I left a note for Mum at the dry cleaner's. Eventually she did come in and the store owner gave her my note.

It had been ten years since she had seen any of her children, so Mum needed some time to come to grips with me making contact. It took her about three weeks to call me, but we arranged to meet at the Regent Hotel near Circular Quay.

When I first saw Mum that day I was amazed that she looked exactly the same to me as she had ten years earlier. I was so happy to see her, but from the way she was searching my face, I could see that she was looking for the eight-year-old, not the eighteen-year-old. She did not recognise me.

I was swimming against a current of unbelievably painful emotions. I wanted Mum to reach out to me, scoop me up and hold me close, but she could only search for the lost girl that she remembered from ten years ago. How gruelling! It was like talking to a wall; she was simply a beautiful facade. I guess this was how she tried to protect herself after spending so long trying to see us without success. I couldn't reach her. It was so distressing to feel rejected like this after all the effort I had put into finding her.

All I wanted was a friend to share moments with. We were almost like strangers, no connection except a polite interaction. Now I know that this was my mother's survival strategy, she simply distanced herself from life.

She was the same way in her relationships with men, existing only on the surface, caring for their every need, looking good and never wanting any emotional connection. In these days of high stress, the men did not delve deeper to find something they were not missing. In many ways she was the ideal partner.

In later years, Mum told me she invented a trick ankle for those times when she could not keep the façade together. She would go away for a few hours and cry and then blame her sore ankle. I tried to imagine the strain and self-control this life must have held for her. No wonder I could not connect with her, there simply was no way in.

My nature is such that I never give up. I kept going back to Mum over and over. I was always trying to rebuild the relationship that I so vividly remembered from childhood. I wanted to live that dream again. We had other separations over the years, but after each one, something would happen and I would keep going back.

Years later, when I was planning my wedding, I was all knotted up inside trying to figure out if I should invite my mum or not – if I did invite her, would she ruin my day? I tried to think about it from her point of view. Would she ever have the opportunity to see one of her four children get married? After four months of agonising thought and many talks with my sister, I decided to invite my mum. My sister was so proud of me for doing that.

I could see that Mum was different at my wedding, but I didn't know what had changed in her. We were walking on the beach in Byron Bay when I confronted her, 'Why did you never contact me, never call, never write? Nothing. I am your child. What happened?' Mum said later that at that moment, she heard a voice saying, 'Just let it all go and love this girl.'

This was the start of a heartfelt relationship with Mum. It was the start of our becoming friends and in some way it was the start of me putting all the pieces of a very fractured puzzle together. The friendship that we developed from this point far exceeded my expectations of what was possible in a relationship with my 'closed' mother. I am so glad I made that incredibly hard decision to invite my mother to my wedding.

Later, when I spent many years living in Canada, Mum phoned me regularly and sent me letters every week about her feelings, about the love she had begun to allow herself to feel. She had some sadness for the lost years, but was willing to make up for them.

She is so opposite to me, I am a hippy at heart, while she is a structured being with a love of classy shoes and handbags. All we can do about it is laugh; sometimes that's the only way.

- Chapter Eight -
My Dad, Larger Than Life

"To understand everything is to forgive everything."

Buddha

One of the gifts Dad gave me was the ability to take life by the horns and just go for it. Of course, this philosophy can be both negative and positive. One thing I'm not so good at is waiting. This habit of diving into things without planning has taught me that it's not always good to dive. When you land on your head you can hurt yourself!

Dad was a mix of so many people: he was a player, doctor and multi-lingual pilot. He was larger than life and every colour of the rainbow. I loved Dad's charisma, charm and humour, and admired his passion and skill for his profession. However, one thing he wasn't was a father.

Dad came from a line of blue-collar workers from Pontypridd, a lower middle class town in Wales. My grandfather was a builder and my great-grandfather was a coal miner. Dad broke the mould to become the first person in his family to finish high school. He even got into university, by using his rugby skills.

Although I never met my grandfather, everyone spoke of him with admiration. He had loads of integrity and was very community-focused. When he died, he left a good portion of his money to a wide variety of charities, pretty much bypassing Dad in his will. I guess he was smarter than we all knew, because when Dad died it came out that he was a big gambler. Maybe my grandfather knew this and was protecting his hard-earned money.

Dad signed up for World War II and became a Lancaster Bomber pilot. Although he never spoke about it, many years later Mum told me something about Dad's experiences during the war; stories of him setting out on missions and never knowing which of his team would come back, and about the time he turned to talk to his co-pilot only to find him dead, riddled with bullet holes. What an effect this must have had on Dad.

It is said that the average lifespan of a bomber pilot was only four weeks, and that over 55,000 English bomber pilots lost their lives in the war. It's amazing with those kinds of statistics that my father's genes managed to live on.

A testament to his luck in survival is the story of his crash-landing his plane when the landing gear didn't come down. The co-pilot died instantly, as he was catapulted out of the cockpit through a window no bigger than a rabbit hutch. My six-foot three dad must have wondered, 'Why him and not me?' Dad's back was damaged in seven places in the crash, and he was never the same afterwards. He lost a few inches in height that day, and the odd ounce of courage. I remember him being in a lot of pain throughout my childhood, living on tablets and enemas, but he never talked about what happened.

He was a stubborn man and always had to be right. Whenever he told a story, he believed his memory of events was correct, no matter what anyone else said. Although it could be hard to deal with, I could see that this came from insecurity. Even now, my family say that of all the children, I am most like my dad, with all the pros and cons!

Dad was quite an eccentric, and drove to work every day at around ten miles an hour. His parrot, Harry, who had a broken wing, would hold onto the hood ornament on the bonnet of the car all the way there. When they arrived at the surgery, Harry would march through the back door, through the waiting room, out the front door and hop up into his favourite tree. The patients often wouldn't notice a small bird wandering through the surgery, but they sure noticed the doctor charging after him, searching the tree and shouting, 'Harry, get down from there now!' I'm sure the little old ladies in the waiting room would twitter amongst themselves, 'I think the doctor has finally lost his marbles.'

My dad had six children from three different wives, as well as one son he adopted with his first wife. Mum tells me that after her second child, he told her that he really did not like children, and didn't want them. I never had a close relationship with my dad, and didn't feel I really knew him. Although Mum said that when I was born, Dad had said, 'She is mine', I never felt the connection, or any interest from him.

When he died, I thought it was sad but it was not really a loss. I never felt the urge to connect with Dad as I had with Mum. As a child, I had seen him almost every day, but he remained a stranger. I can't recall a serious conversation with him, about him, about his past, what he was thinking, or what he was feeling. Maybe the war deadened him to all that. Perhaps it also deadened him to the people around him. This affected all of us in one way or another. I often wonder, if I had known more about him while he was alive, could things have been different?

- Chapter Nine -
See Me Fly

*"A good traveller has no fixed plans,
and is not intent on arriving."*

Lao Tzu

My adopted brother, Stuart from Dad's first marriage, came to visit us at our home in Cudgen when I was eleven. He was on a break from his studies in America. 'Wow', I thought, 'another country. That's exciting.' I decided then and there that I wanted to get a university degree and then go travelling. And that's exactly what I did.

Although I had really wanted to study to be a physical education teacher, Dad felt that wasn't good enough for our family. He had me psychologically tested and the results indicated that I should study business or physiotherapy. When I was younger, I had always wanted to be a stage actor. I thought this was self-indulgent, so I put the thought away; although the desire to act would stay with me forever, quietly in the corner of my soul, just waiting for the right time to appear.

In the meantime, I enrolled in a business degree at the University of Technology in Sydney. Although I made great friends and had a phenomenal social life during my time there, I hated the course, and only the fear of my father stopped me from changing over to physical education. Twice, I came close to switching courses, but each time I could not find the courage to tell my dad so I didn't go through with it.

The business degree was pretty full-on. I majored in marketing and industrial relations, and studied full time while nannying for a family at Potts Point. I cared for three children, aged two, five and seven, for food and board, and if I worked on the weekends as well I made a little bit of extra pocket money. This didn't leave enough time for full time study, and after six months I had failed four out of six subjects and was on probation.

I needed to get marks of fifty plus for all my subjects in the next semester, or I would not be allowed to stay at university. I put in a big effort but was disappointed to see that I had only made it to fifty or fifty one. I knew then that I needed to take drastic action, and at nineteen years old I packed in full time university in favour of full time work. I continued my studies, but only part time. This turned out to be a great choice.

Working full time at Colgate-Palmolive in marketing, university classes three nights a week and projects on weekends seemed to work for my personality, and my marks started to sky-rocket. I had always been someone to pile a lot on my plate, and my overflowing stores of energy had to be used up somehow.

Once I finished university, I worked for six months for the Minister of the Environment in the Public Relations Department. I learned a lot about the power of public relations, and also saved up for my much-anticipated overseas trip.

- Chapter Ten -

Travel Diary Of A
20 Something Year Old Girl

"A journey of a thousand miles starts with a single step."

Mao Tse Tung

It's September and Cassie and I are sharing
a cheap motel room, $12 bucks a night.
Almost free. We had to do it, yesterday in
Yellowstone Park we couldn't open our tent
zipper. Frozen solid. Had to make a hole to
wriggle through, so tonight it's luxury.
A warm bed, no zippers.

Yellowstone. How do you describe something
as beautiful as Yellowstone? The most
wondrous wildlife. I just couldn't take
enough pictures. Oh so very awesome.
Originally we were only going to drive through
but our visit turned into a day. Old Faithful,
the geyser, was so spectacular; the steam
from the geysers had sulphur in it, so it
smelled a bit like rotten eggs. On the way out
we had dinner at a café and met two of the
smoothest guys you could imagine. Swedish
and absolutely unbelievable. To stay or not to
stay. We tore away. Yes!

Lots of bikers passed us yesterday, giving
us curious looks, we are so underdressed
in hoodies and overalls. One actually
stopped and had a good look at our car,
then blew wind and told us it was just a
piece of crap. So?

Then another night in the tent, and breakfast on the car hood, at least that was warm, and then a sponge bath in a service station. We were living it up.

Next day we were going to Cape Canaveral to see space shuttles and all those very interesting things, always on the news, we had to see it firsthand.

The space centre was very interesting, but as I'd been to the Air and Space Museum, there was a fair bit of overlap. A space shuttle was due to be launched this day or the next. I saw those huge transporter crawlers which moved the shuttles. So very slow. I guess those shuttles are quite heavy. You would have more fun watching grass grow than watching those shuttles move.

So there we were travelling all the way down to the south end of the states. Somewhere along the way, we decided to go to New Orleans - or "Norlens" as the locals call it. Cassie and I thought it might be a good idea to learn about local flora and fauna so we decided that we wanted to do this alligator tour - like in the swamps. The guy who was our guide was as black as tar at midnight. Back home in Australia in the city, I just had not seen anyone alive this dark. They were so black, they were almost purple. Anyway, I am losing the plot here - 'cause I want to tell you a story - a very funny story about us learning about alligators and one hellish night that I did not sleep. Talk about letting my mind race away with me!... Here is the story...

We were driving along and getting pretty tired - there is a lot of road to cover in the states. So Cassie was starting to get sleepy and as she always drove - I usually slept in the back of the car - I got a lot of sleep in those 4 months. Cassie like never slept so of course she drove! Anyway, our headlights being as dim as they were, we could not see that much ahead - I thought that we should pull over. We couldn't see and Cassie was tired. The smart thing to do was to stop. So...

We needed a place to put the tent up that night, as we had driven right across three states. All we needed was a stretch of flat grass that would hold a tent. Cassie pulled the car over and we popped the boot, got the tent out and slapped it up. We threw the mattresses and sleeping bags in and were soon fast asleep, or at least she was. No sooner had we hit the hay then I heard noises outside the tent. I woke Cassie up and I said 'Can you hear that?' She mumbled for me to go back to sleep, but I was sure that someone was trying to jimmy our padlock to get into our $400 car. Looking back, what was I thinking? That someone wanted to steal our billy to make their tea? There was very little anyone could want in that car. Anyway, I was on edge by then so there was no sleep for me, I was wide awake. About thirty minutes later, I heard another noise, louder this time, and I vigorously shook Cassie 'You must have heard that!' I said. 'What?' she moaned. Pretty soon, she got really annoyed. 'Hissing!' I said, 'I can hear hissing.'

On our swamp tour, we were told that alligators hiss while they sleep. The sound was really close to our tent now and I was imagining those alligators with their big choppers that could bite right though our side flaps. Cassie said again, 'Go to sleep'. I was really tired, but just lay there, wide awake. Next I heard a really big bang. I rolled over to her and yelled right in her ear 'You must have heard that!'. She replied grumpily, 'If you are so worried, why don't you take a look?' I didn't want to go out there on my own, so I had to just lie there. There was no sleep for me that night. I lay on my mattress 'til dawn, counting buzzing mossies outside the tent and hoping that we would not be eaten, bashed or broken into.

The next morning, Cassie finally awoke, fresh as a daisy. I poked my head out of the tent, and this time the zipper whizzed down gleefully. I couldn't see what had been making the noise, but noticed something else interesting. 'Cassie, check this out, you have got to see this!'

We had actually driven right into someone's back yard and were camped at the edge of their property. I can imagine the conversation those homeowners were having: 'Honey, did you put a tent in the back yard recently? Or are we expecting the grandkids?' If I had more gusto, I would have walked

up to the front door and asked for some
bacon and eggs, it seemed pretty funny
in my mind. We felt a little sheepish for
intruding right into someone's property, so
we thought it best to quietly pack up and
manoeuvre our heavy tank back out of there.
Back to the highway and then onwards and
upwards for the next adventure.

We were driving on to DC and stopped at
Buck Lake to camp. Nice. Watched David
Letterman, what a scream!

Next day we drove all the way from Buck
Lake in one of the Carolinas to DC, arriving
at about 10 am. It was great to see Stuart
and Barbara again and give them a brief
run-down of our wondrous adventures.
All those photographs, old mail and lost
stories. We were up until 2 am, with an
early start in the morning.

When we stopped at a Burger King the next
day, we saw this hitchhiker. He looked OK,
so we decided to pick him up. We also
decided to liven up our own stories, camping
and frozen zippers and indifferent bikers can
only go so far.

So Cassie became Sky and I was Jemima.
Sky had two sisters, Summer and Rain and
her parents had been to Woodstock. Of
course. My story was simple – my father
was Wayne Gardner and he travelled the
world racing. Well, the hitchhiker bought it
all. He was a musician. That's why.

Next day was Saturday. On those world
trips we made, one day was as good as

the next, but one day had to be veg-out day, so this was it. Next day was Sunday. Thyme came over and Stuart changed the oil in our car. Painted a bit more, went to Laurie's and met her parents. Watched The 4th of July and cried. Another long night. Those nights in DC were such long ones.

One more day on. Had to do some shopping and in the afternoon we met Barb Farthing and his friend 'Herb'. We kept them entertained with our stories and they thought we were crackers. Herb took a shine to Cassie and decided to come to Vancouver. Who says three is a crowd?

To feel more human, Cassie waxed her legs the next day and I had a facial. Picked up our photos from Lake Tahoe. Great shots. Then we drove to Cassie's friend Sarah's place. She lived in Virginia. It was so beautiful.

We ended up going to Old Town in Virginia after a great meal and excellent conversation with Sarah's parents. After a good night's sleep we left at a reasonable hour, driving to Allentown in Pennsylvania.

We stopped at Annapolis and had some special chips. They are 1/4 potatoes and you put some salt, vinegar and bay spices on them. Wow.

What should have taken four hours to travel took nearly nine hours. We really messed up here. The road directions were almost impossible to see, let alone read. We actually went through three states,

New Jersey, Delaware and Pennsylvania, before we got to Allentown. Just the usual short, scenic tour. We ended up camping at Quaker Town since uncle Don and Ruthie Allen had visitors.

Well, today we got to Ruthie and Uncle Don's, even though Cassie was a bit worried about her reception. It was better than she expected. They were absolutely lovely. Kept the food and alcohol coming. How hospitable.

We stayed up talking, there was Nelleck, and Geoff from Perth, old friends of Cassie's from her gymnastics course, some years ago. Stu was quite crude because he was wealthy and could do what he liked. Ruthie was one of the sweetest ladies one could meet, always making everything nice, right, warm and cosy. Don was cute and you could see he had been a bit of a rebel in his day.

We decided to drive to New York the next day. It would have been a pity not to go, since we were so close.

New York, New York. What a place. To visit, to see, to spend time. But not to live. At least not for me. It is an awesome place.

Statue of Liberty, Metropolitan Museum of Modern Art, Empire State Building, Madison Square Gardens, Soho, Queens, The Bronx, Eastern Subway, The Rockefeller Centre, Twin Towers, Wall Street, Broadway, Times Square, The Hard-Rock Café, Café 43, Grand Central Station 43rd, Roosevelt Island.

We got up really early so we could see

as much as possible. Caught the 7.30 am from Allentown to New York. About an hour and a bit. When we got there we walked the length of Manhattan, Soho and part of Greenwich Village to the World Trade Centre. Awesome. We got a great view of the city.

After that, Cassie forced me to meet Chris. He was an old boyfriend I had dated at university. My friend had met three American exchange students and somehow – I don't know how – we started dating them. One American guy for each Australian girl, it was convenient. I was very nervous and thought it was a really stupid idea to meet up with him again. Anyway, he hadn't changed a bit, except lost a lot more weight. I was very quiet, but Cassie fell in love with him. Anyway, for some reason I was glad I saw him, even though it definitely killed me. After that we caught the subway to The Hard-Rock Café. I was a bit worried about maybe getting stuck in the subway.

When we got to The Hard-Rock Café we had a $50 lunch. Boy, is NY expensive. It was really only sandwiches and a Hurricane, which I might add, I finished. Then it was off to the Metro Museum of Art.

We are into October now. Went to the Rockette's gym, Cassie being a bit of a gymnastics freak, made me go. Yep! Forward roll, backward roll, forward again. I wonder if that reflected Cassie's thoughts. Finally even Cassie had enough.

Cried a parting tear, squeezed Julie's huge frame and I put my foot flat to the floor to get away from those rolls as fast as possible.

We drove all night to arrive in Chicago at about 2 am. Joe had come back from the Canyon and Vegas, said he had had a great time. He didn't think I would come and stay, but we did and had another night of fun and excitement.

Sunday, early October. Joe took us out for a great breakfast and we didn't leave 'til about 12 noon. Drove all day through Nebraska, gone in a flash.

Driving more next day, we were on a road trip after all. Blew a radiator hose, but luckily were close to a service station. Well, Cassie and I had another one of our brawls. I was a bit put off when she tried to tell me how she would pay me back the money she owed me. I was annoyed, she was annoyed, but we were travelling together, so? I guess it was a lose-lose situation. I don't think we made conversation except about directions. Then to top off this day, we slept in our tent in Riverton and it froze. Do you believe it? The zip froze again and we had to make a hole again. Yes!

It was just on autumn and the leaves were starting to turn every shade of orange, burnt red, yellow and ochre. The autumn leaves are one of the beauties of North America. How could nature produce such exquisite art? It does something to you on the inside. I wanted to drive through the scenery again and again, to experience the emotional reality of the colour changes, and remember them forever.

I loved travelling without a plan. Being as free as a bird and never knowing what new adventure or situation would show up. For many years, I would simply book a ticket to a distant destination and see how the chips fell. It was always so exciting; I liked the thrill of the unknown as much as being part of the cultures and lives that I travelled to and with.

Most days on the road through the USA, our only decision was whether or not to go left or right, and even then we struggled to make up our minds. We forgot responsibility, duty, daily necessities, we just were. Life rolled into miles and miles of thick black tar, sometimes with lines, sometimes with no lines. Thousands of kilometres of open road which seemed not to lead anywhere. I was able to get to know myself well with all that time driving along those long, quiet open roads.

We decided to stay at another cheap motel and I walked into a storeroom by mistake. Luckily I scored a blanket and some towels.

Well, it's New Year's Eve. End of the year. I cannot believe it. A monumental eight months have passed in the breeze of what seems like a second.

- Chapter Eleven -
Deja Vu In Canada

"I would rather regret the things I have done than the things I have not."

Lucille Ball

Cassie and I spent a week in Vancouver in an incredible youth hostel with 400 beds, and then drove on to Whistler.

Whistler was unlike any other town we had visited so far. We both knew immediately that we would be staying a while. I'd never been there before, but it felt familiar to me. The architecture was magnificent. Some of the houses were like works of art, with Inuit statements carved into their front doors.

The landscape was magical; so beautiful, with staggering sheer, stark mountains that looked as if they could tumble into the valley at any time.

Whistler was a small town of only around 10,000 people, so it seemed that everybody knew everybody else. But what a population they were! Whistler was filled with extraordinarily talented and very alive people.

High profile sports people, world explorers, backcountry skiers, musicians, artists; all kinds of extreme people were attracted to Whistler. People who made a lot of money and cared about their spirit and their body, and of course the regular backpackers and students who literally had nothing except the shirts on their backs. People who wanted to live extraordinary lives.

The businesses reflected the lifestyle of the people who were drawn there. There were a few organic and vegan food stores and alternative health practitioners, and even a Steiner school. There were ten or fifteen psychics in town. For a small town, that's a lot of psychics!

We stayed on the floor of Rico's place, a friend of mine from university. Rico lived in staff housing at the Whistler Blackcomb Ski Resort. Soon we got our own room right across the hall. It was party central, and the hallways were always full of young, beautiful travellers who'd come to work and play in the snow.

Cassie landed a nanny job and started to go her own way, meeting guys and having fun. I worked in a bakery for a while, where I learned to make great clam chowder, but soon moved on to waitressing as there were about 150 restaurants in Whistler.

I'd get up early each morning to ski all day, then work until about 2 am, then go partying. Then a short sleep and do it all over again. Soon I had skied 100 days in a row and partied that many too!

I met Harry at an Australia Day party. He had blue eyes, blonde hair and was very cool. He was four inches shorter than me, three years younger than me, and worked in another restaurant. He had attended a high school for elite snow athletes in Virginia, and this demonstration of excellence really appealed to me.

After six months of wooing me in the old fashioned way, with endless roses and champagne, he finally wore me down. I agreed to go out with him. He took me skiing on one of our first dates, and had the opportunity to show me what an incredibly talented skier he was. I confused loving watching him ski with falling in love with him, and within a few weeks we were living together.

About seven of us shared a multi million dollar mansion. You had to have an official address to work in Whistler, and with so many people wanting to work there, accommodation was hard to find. Cassie's room was a cupboard under the stairs. Yes, a cupboard!

Harry held the lease to this house so he was able to choose the best room. It was just gorgeous, with a balcony and ensuite. Although I wasn't really in love, living together made it feel permanent. I didn't think I would marry him or indeed anyone else, I just couldn't see myself making that commitment, but I didn't want to hurt his feelings by telling him I didn't love him, so I stayed. I guess I was hoping to find someone to share my dreams and enjoy life with me, but I was in a fairly fractured state and just could not conceive this was really possible.

Harry began to have more and more control over me and soon I started to feel that I couldn't breathe or be myself. I had been in Canada for about nine months and was starting to miss my friends, family and lifestyle back home in Australia.

I was fed up with being a waitress. Being so subservient to others was just not me. Smiling, wiping tables, filling glasses, wiping cutlery, smiling, wiping tables. I called myself 'The Beer Slinging Girl From Hell'. I could not stand it another minute. I had to have space to think, to be free. I had made good money as a waitress and saved all my tips, so Cassie and I hopped back into our old car and headed for Alaska.

I knew by now that I had control over what I did with my time. I knew that if I wanted to be free and wander around the world, all I had to do was to organise my life to make it happen.

The scenery was just stunning as we drove the 1500 miles to the Alaskan border. On the way, we took a ferry ride onto a beautiful lake. The lake was truly breathtaking, an azure blue colour that somehow didn't look real. I had heard that the colour had something to do with how the sun strikes the silt run-off from the glacier. Travelling meant I was learning wild facts every day!

The ferry stopped for a short time so we could take in the lake's unique beauty. In that place, I felt a sense of wholeness. It was so tranquil. I didn't want any distractions, so while the others stayed by the ferry, I walked up the hill and sat alone to look down on the lake. The water looked like glass, there wasn't a ripple on the surface. I felt truly at peace in that moment.

We camped in Kluane at a campsite that apparently had the highest concentration of grizzly bears in the state. What a drawcard for campers! We often saw wild, big horned sheep or goats along the way, giving the journey a real Grizzly Adams feel.

We avoided paying for accommodation by doing a runner. We'd find campsites, pitch our $20 tent, sleep, then by 6 am, before the grounds' offices were open, we would be gone. On the way out we would slap the steering wheel of our car and chastise it for being naughty. 'Naughty car, naughty, naughty car.'

We made the excuse that our budget of $20 a day couldn't stretch to accommodation. I was young, so very young.

Near the Alaskan border, we camped outside Prince Rupert, a small fishing town with some paper mills. It looked like the set of an old movie – everything was made of timber and the people wore flannel and drank constantly. Prince Rupert was the kind of place that prides itself on hard men and even harder women. Cassie and I were looking for some fun, so when we stopped at a bakery we pretended we couldn't speak English. We couldn't keep it up though, and the game ended rather abruptly.

The next great idea was to leave the car in a long-term car park and start hitchhiking. The idea of hitchhiking really appealed to me – it was the perfect way for me to experience a day in the lives of lots of different people. I found this just fascinating. Everyone who picked us up was so kind, we were really incredibly lucky, as so many bad things have happened to hitchhikers. People seemed to be so interested to find out more about the two Australian girls roaming their country, with loads of curiosity and a big appetite for adventure. Hopefully it opened their eyes to the possibilities in their own lives.

We didn't mind where they were headed, as long as it was forward that was OK with us. Sharing their journeys, we were able to experience their way of being, the foods they ate, sometimes the houses they lived in and also the ways they loved and nurtured.

Hitchhiking took us to a roadhouse in Yukon, a luxurious break from camping. Here the crowd was entertained by a very buxom lady playing the spoons. She was wearing a corseted black top over a flouncy gingham check dress, and seemed to be in danger of popping right out of that corset onto someone's plate. Bosom entree! Boy, could she play those spoons well though. Every now and then she would lose one of the spoons down her ample bosom, and I wondered how often she found cutlery in her underwear as she got ready for bed. It reminded me of the way you always find a teaspoon in the sink after you have done the dishes, it doesn't matter how diligent you are with the dishes, there is always a teaspoon in the sink!

- Chapter Twelve -
Hitching Through Alaska

"What you've done becomes the judge of what you're going to do – especially in other people's minds.
When you're travelling,
you are what you are right there and then.
People don't have your past to hold against you.
No yesterdays on the road."

William Least Heat-Moon, Blue Highways

We hitched our way into Alaska, such an immensely old and empty country. It was so wild and raw and the wilderness was unique – acres and acres of trees that were only three feet tall. They were sixty years old but the harsh climate meant they only grew about fifteen millimetres a year. If I grew five millimetres a year, I would be the size of a pygmy! There was a slowness to the whole country; the people seemed as if they were a hundred years behind the rest of America, and still had their good old-fashioned values intact.

We camped near the Mendanhall Glacier and the next morning climbed all around the glacier, under it and over it. The locals later told us how silly this was, as the glacier was not stable. We sat on the rocks beside a stream and watched the salmon as they completed the last leg of their journey against the rushing waters of the river up to the spawning grounds. They jumped over waterfalls two or three feet high, sometimes missing and hitting the rocks, falling momentarily stunned into the water. The salmon were almost a red colour by this part of the journey, and we watched with awe and even a kind of recognition as they urged themselves forward, exhausted and delirious, towards their destiny.

As we got closer to Anchorage, the most remote city in

the world, our rides became smaller. We were picked up by two tiny little ladies in two tiny little cars. The second tiny little lady invited us to stay with her for the night and fed us hearty meals of home-grown eggs and veges. She was a teacher, and sat chatting for hours in her cat's eye glasses, glad for the company.

It was raining when we set off the next day, and after three hours we still hadn't got a ride. Who would want two girls who looked like drowned rats in their car? I had the brilliant idea to split up. Surely one drowned rat would be less of a problem than two.

We drew straws for the first lift and I won a ride in a truck with a guy with a beard and a beer belly, who only shared the occasional word between his constant spitting, as he was chewing his awful pumpkin seeds. It was a very long drive.

We had made a vague plan to meet up at the next big town, figuring that all the towns had only one main road going through them so we should be able to find each other. We were right, and after a few hours Cassie turned up. Filled with the carefree confidence of youth, we never doubted we would find each other.

I always thought during these travelling adventures that everything would work out. And it did, luckily. I rarely kept in touch with the people at home, so no one would ever know if something had happened to me. Besides, I felt totally unloved. Who was there to care what happened to me? Sometimes I don't think I even cared myself.

Either there was luck on my side, or there were angels looking out for me. Maybe both. The kindness of strangers we constantly encountered warmed my heart and gave me hope. I became rich through these experiences in ways that would not become apparent for years.

Once Cassie and I found each other, our next ride was with John in his removal truck. We drove all day through magical scenery to stop at the awfully named Dead Man's Lake for the night. I think our stop here put Cassie and I a little on edge – we shouldn't have worried, John was a gem. First he bought us Sloppy Joes, which were like spaghetti bolognaise in a bun, and then he made some room in the back of the truck for us to sleep, while he slept underneath. In the morning, he went for a walk and picked an overflowing pail of blueberries for us. What a gentleman.

Our next ride was memorable in a different way, with a guy with no teeth and a flaming red afro hairdo so high it touched the roof of his car. He drove one-handed while he rolled a joint, talking about the famous Woodstock Festival as if it was last weekend. We were as high as kites as we rolled into Anchorage, and wandered aimlessly round and round on the main street in an attempt to find the youth hostel. When we finally found it, we somehow managed to check in and lay giggling on our beds for hours, watching the paint wash across the walls in waves.

From Anchorage we went on to Denali National Park, right in the heart of Alaska, on a shuttle bus through the luscious nature of the park. We set up our tent at Riley Creek campground, where we were lucky enough to see a mamma grizzly bear with her triplets. We wanted to visit Mt McKinley, which we had heard was the coldest mountain in the world and as dangerous as it was cold, but despite waiting for a few days, the dense low-hanging fog wouldn't let us close.

The mountain ranges in Alaska were so very serious, stark and sheer. They were only 8000 or 9000 feet high and sprinkled with caribou and dall sheep with their curved horns. The vegetation was low and stunted, and as we walked we were careful not to crush the tiny white flowers that only bloom briefly every three years. When you are hiking, you are requested not to tread on the same path as someone else. If a flower is trodden on once, it will have a chance to recover and bloom again in the spring. If it is trodden on many times, it probably will not make it.

I watched some dog sled demonstrations and Cassie went river rafting, then we headed towards Prudhoe Bay, which is famous for its high suicide rate. Luckily, we didn't make it all the way there.

This whole area is affected by Seasonal Affected Disorder. The days are very short in the winter, but for eight weeks in summer there is light 24 hours a day. The sun literally makes a perfect circle as it travels around and around the horizon, and it can be very disorientating. We had a debate coming down from a hike, when we ran into some other hikers who were going up. We thought it was 3 pm, but they assured us it was 3 am. No wonder we were so tired! With all the sunlight, your body tells you that there are things to do and people to play with, even when you are tired. Companies have to offer staff bonus money to work there, but I don't think it would be worth it!

During our four months around Alaska we contemplated travelling overland to Russia. By the end, though, we were tired and running out of money, so we decided to hitchhike back to our car, and were soon driving back to Whistler.

- Chapter Thirteen -
Developing A Taste For Travel

*"I just wish the world was twice as big
and half of it was still unexplored."*

David Attenborough

Cassie and I went back to our rooms at the mansion, and I went back to my co-dependent relationship with Harry. Over the next four years we would break up many times. Rather than having the courage to leave, I foolishly waited and watched the relationship slowly fragment until there wasn't even a friendship left.

After Alaska, our money was fairly tight, so Cassie and I had let our car's registration lapse. The police pulled us over and impounded our car. We didn't have enough money to get it back out, so the police crushed our special painted car. It was very sad, that car had taken us so far and we had so many unforgettable memories attached to it.

After a few months, I was ready to move on again. Whistler had a very transient population and didn't offer me the stability I inwardly craved. It was hard to establish friendships, as most people didn't stay for long.

With a growing taste for foreign places, I started to save to go to Europe, where both my parents came from. Perhaps I was looking for my roots, or perhaps I just wanted to see as many places as I could and immerse myself in as many cultures as possible.

Cassie had decided to stay on in Whistler, so Harry and I headed off together. We took a one-way hire car to Quebec City, then on to New York for our flights to Europe. Quebec was quite a city. Although the rest of Canada goes to great pains to label everything bilingually,

Quebec has its own ideas. Everything was in French. My French is very limited, so what should have been a ten minute trip out of the city ended up being a two and a half hour journey. I simply did not know enough French to leave the city.

- Chapter Fourteen -
A Stolen Heart

"You love simply because you cannot help it."
Kim Anderson

I had met Sebastian way back when I was living in Whistler in 1990, while I was dating Harry.

We were at the local watering hole, Citta's. Sebastian was Australian, tall and painfully thin, with thick dark unkempt hair, and deep-set, dark blue eyes. He wore a feather earring – I could never decide if this was cool, spiritual, or just a whim. His laugh was full and very old, like a ninety-year-old man enjoying a belly laugh. It was the laugh of someone who had seen it all, great pain and great joy.

The summer beer lulled me into love and I knew I needed to get to know this man, even though I was already with Harry.

Sebastian and I saw each other often, as good friends. Somehow I never felt good enough for him. He constantly laughed at my quirky ways and that laugh had an air of wisdom and knowing, always making me feel that I had just done something silly or childish. I knew he was important to me, because I would squirm physically when I was with him, but felt so overwhelmed that I could not even consider sleeping with him.

As my relationship with Harry deteriorated, we would be out for dinner and in between courses, I would call Sebastian. I needed Sebastian. But I did not know how to have him and still couldn't bring myself to break up with Harry.

We would have the most amazing conversations, covering so many topics. We talked like a sea anemone branches over the ocean floor trying to feel its surroundings. One year we talked every single day. I have never had this depth of communication with another human.

We were never more than good friends, but we were in love with each other for many years. Whenever one of us wanted to act on those feelings, the other one would be in a relationship. He lived in Whistler for a while, then Hong Kong, then Sydney, but never at the right time. We were like ships in the night, forever passing each other but never meeting.

We did know each other intimately many years later and it was worth the wait when it finally happened, but the relationship was doomed from the start. Although I eventually let go of him, Sebastian is still tucked away in a safe place in my heart, with a fluffy doona and a hot water bottle in case it gets chilly.

– Chapter Fifteen –
A Poem For My Love

*"What the heart gives away is never gone
It is kept in the hearts of others."*

Robin St. John

For Sebastian.

If you were the wind I would be the trees, so that I could feel you as you moved through my leaves, tousling and playing with them on your way to distant lands.

If I were the sand dunes and you were the breeze, I would let your billowy hotness shape my dunes and allow my sand to flow all over the world. I would allow my river of sand to fall away, trickling into a fine mist, drifting off by itself like a silk shawl from a beautiful lady's shoulders.

If you were the ocean, I would be a dolphin, playing and diving and leaping through your swirling energy, enjoying your coolness. When you were serene I could swim for miles and see all there was to see. When your waters turned into a foaming salty dog, I would brave your crashing shores to see what I could see.

I would be part of you, you part of me and our togetherness a natural symbiosis. If I were a seahorse, then you would be my mate, because when one seahorse dies so too does the other one.

If I were a flower then you would be my sunshine, moonlight, rain and shade. I would stretch towards you in the hope of one day reaching my source. My smiley face of petals would light the hearts of all who beheld me and I would be a wonder to behold. My essence, my nature, I would trust in your hands.

*If I were your lover, your life partner, your soul mate,
sex kitten and best friend, I would listen to all
that you shared.*

*I would take the time to give you honest and true
feedback and focus on you and your communication
rather than the voice inside my head that is consumed
with me. I would take care with your words and their
meaning and respect your voice. I would offer you my
interpretation from a place of love, wanting to know you
and help you on your soulful journey.*

I would lovingly touch you often and much.

*You would know how much I cared for you by my touch,
no matter where we were.*

*When I see your face my heart smiles and shines
through my eyes and you know I love you.*

I would be calm and present when you most needed it

*I would make you tea in the morning and
bring it to you in bed*

I would tickle your fancy

I would make you smile

And laugh

And sometimes cry, but hopefully not often

*I would treasure each and every moment
we spent together*

I would plan adventures with you

I would grow with you

Read with you and

Learn with you

*I would make love with you in the morning
and sometimes in the night*

*I would hold your hand and run with you
(hopefully not far!)*

*I would remember all the small things about you
that really count*

*That you are shy when you can't express yourself
and you need some time*

That you like it slow
That you need to be heard
That your mind is always thinking
That you care and you are loving
That you desire to be loved, physically, emotionally,
spiritually and most of all mentally
That you are visual
That you trust me
That you have an impressive and extraordinary mind
That you are old-fashioned and worldly, together
That you love beautiful cars
If I truly cared ... all of this I would know

What should have, could have, but never was.

- Chapter Sixteen -
Grey, Grey And More Grey — Britain

"I dislike feeling at home when I'm abroad."
George Bernard Shaw

London. A little blurry. Wet, slushy and grey. It was winter and I was trying to distance myself from this on-again off-again love affair with Harry. I couldn't seem to let go of this co-dependent relationship and kept sipping at it like a really bad drug, even though I knew it was slowly sucking the life out of me and eroding my soul.

Each time we broke up we would find our way back together, drawn to each other like tiny balls of mercury, but just as toxic. I was scared to be alone, so I stayed in it for the identity it gave me, feeling safe in the knowledge that Harry loved me. It was my first serious relationship and he was very controlling, although he didn't appear to know it. They say you marry one of your parents and I think I was in a relationship with both of mine. In many ways, Harry was my stepmother and my dad all rolled into one, not a great combination.

It seemed that while we were in the mountains our relationship worked. Just. When our relationship was anywhere else it didn't work. There was nothing to hold it together except snow, yet that too had melted.

After the beauty of Canada, London was hard to get used to. So grey, all the time. How could people smile in this place? The greyness seeped right into my soul until I felt dampness on the inside. I wondered if my soul was subject to mould. The markets were fantastic and there was always something happening on the streets and in the pubs. But still, it was grey.

There was so much to see and our money was getting low.

Our $20 daily budget was impossible to keep to in London.

On to Wales, so I could see Pontypridd, where my Dad came from. Those Welsh road signs were crazy. Who could pronounce the town name: Llanfairpwllgwyngyll-gogerchwyrndrobwllllantysiliogogogoch? Even the Welsh people couldn't say it, they had to shorten it to Llanfair-pwll. Apparently the short name is pronounced *thlan vire puth*. Even that made my tongue hurt.

We drove up to Rosslare Harbour and caught the ferry to Dublin. Ireland was lovely but our visit was too brief. We sat in a pub drinking Guinness, listening to the locals talk. Their Irish accents were as thick as mist and I didn't understand a word they were saying, so all I could do was smile and nod. I must have looked pretty absurd.

- Chapter Seventeen -
Seeing The World

"Travel at its truest is thus an ironic experience and the best travellers seem to be those able to hold two or three inconsistent ideas in their minds at the same time or able to regard themselves as at once serious persons and clowns."

Paul Fussell

From Rosslare Harbour, Harry and I took the ferry to Cherbourg in France. The ferry was full of Americans travelling around Europe. They were so friendly, once they discovered I spoke English. It was easy to tell American travellers by the way they looked, and particularly their footwear. They all seemed to wear a very similar type of white trainer. I wondered why – I knew there was more than one shoe store in America! From Cherbourg we took the train to Paris.

Paris, where everything was so settled, so old, so established, so classy! My cut off jeans and tie-dyed t-shirts were no match for a place like this.

There didn't seem to be an ugly woman in Paris. The women there behaved so discreetly and quietly. Everything matched: the shoes, the bags, the scarves and the earrings. They were like graduates from a Vogue magazine. It seemed to be something they didn't even have to think about, it was just part of their Parisian DNA.

I thought it must have a lot to do with growing up in an atmosphere of style and age-old tradition, and the settled upbringing that a long history brings. We in the new countries are still so set on proving ourselves. Hardly any history, hardly any background, just a couple of centuries of infant steps, trying to find our identity, populated by thieves and sailors.

There were so many things to see that a day bus tour was just a drop in the ocean. The Louvre, with the glass pyramid outside, and inside those priceless paintings and art. It's amazing what man is capable of and amazing what he is incapable of. I think my mouth was open permanently trying to take it all in. I actually saw the REAL Mona Lisa. WOW! What a fantastic life on a shoestring.

To get back to earth I had a French hamburger. Would you believe they put fries on their burgers and hotdogs? I mean ON it! Another strange tradition is that if you are not married by the time you are twenty five, they throw a party for you. Why is that? To congratulate or commiserate I wonder?

Harry and I wandered across France by bus. We sipped Pernod in Marseilles, which I didn't care for. Aniseed and milk, not a great combination. We were refused entry to the casino in Monte Carlo because of my cut-off camouflage shorts. We went on to the incredible mountains of Chamonix, where there was no snow, but they did have postcards which showed what it should have looked like. We decided to take the train to see the countryside. I am sure it was very beautiful, but we had taken the Bullet train and it went so fast that the fields whizzed by in a blur.

Harry and I stayed with a friend who was studying English in Aix. Aix was my favourite place in France, so quaint and seemingly untouched since the 1600s. Harry and I broke up again here, when I accused him of ogling my friend. I packed my backpack and walked out, all on my lonesome, with hardly any money and very little French. Oh well. I went to a bar, had a drink and met a lovely girl I could stay with until I figured out my next travel move.

Switzerland seemed like it would provide some relief for my bruised heart, so I travelled to Montreux and Chillon Castle. It was built on rocks which had been occupied by Bronze Age men. Romans had taken over occupation, then bishops, then counts. Who next?

On I travelled to Gimmelwald. So quaint, I swear Heidi must have been hiding in there somewhere amongst all the cowbells. Here I found the most beautiful youth hostel in the world – perched on top of a mountain.

What a life I had, so full of freedom and no responsibility. Of course I was too young to appreciate this. It's true that youth is wasted on the young.

On my twenty fourth birthday I was travelling through Germany, sitting on a train all day with a sticker with the number twenty four firmly stuck to my forehead. People stared, probably thinking there was something wrong with me. I acted as if it was completely normal – doesn't everyone wear a sticker on their forehead when it is their birthday?

I was heading to Auschwitz in Poland but had to go to Kotowice first to change trains. Shortly after the German/Polish border, two Polish girls joined me and we spent all night trying to learn each other's languages. Polish is such a mouthful, but the night passed quickly.

We arrived at Kotowice at 4 am. I didn't have enough Polish money for the train to Auschwitz, so one of the girls lent me the money for the ticket. I was so grateful. When we arrived in Auschwitz two hours later, the money exchange was not open yet. When it finally opened, the girl at the counter saw my traveller's cheques and said 'Banco'. So I walked around town in the rain, wet and hungry trying to find a 'Banco'. I happened across the entrance to Auschwitz, so I decided to take off my backpack and tour the museum.

The smell of death hung thickly, it was overwhelming. I felt sick, that humans could have done this to each other. War or no war, it was simply incomprehensible.

I met a woman who took me to another money exchange, where we still had no luck. I would have to wait until Monday, then travel to Krakau where one could change traveller's cheques. It was only Saturday. I was a little depressed. I had two bags of dried soup and some paper pouches of coffee. How was I to stretch this over three days?

The woman showed me to some barracks that had

been converted to a hotel. At the entrance of the hotel a German guy was watching the traffic. We struck up a conversation and he took me to another youth hostel where I was able to get a free meal. I was grateful for the meal, but couldn't wait for the time to pass so I could get out of that town. The weight of the history of that town was too hard to handle, my heart felt like it would cave in on itself.

On Monday, I was out of there, to Krakau to change my money, and then on a train to Prague in what was then Czechoslovakia. Huge stoic looking train guards constantly checked my passport and tickets along the way. Once in Prague, I stuffed my backpack into a train station locker and took a bus tour of the city, which was the cheapest way to see everything. The bus took me to the National Museum, then a Somusola, which is an unusual kind of stand-up eatery, then to the Christmas markets.

The next day, I explored another of Europe's endless castles, then Karlovy Vary, the home of the famous Bohemian crystal. I couldn't resist buying a set of wine and port glasses and shipping them home, so pretty and delicate. More shopping at the stalls around a stone bridge older then Methuselah, where they were selling caviar and obsolete USSR Lenin badges.

Onward, ever onward. Next stop East Germany, where I had a chance to see socialism first hand, before the unification. Everyone had a job, which should have been great but actually just led to inefficiency, with four or five people doing the job of one. Low unemployment was of course desirable, but not this way. The lack of competition weakened the economy, and the standard of living was very low. There were secret service and police everywhere. The country had much beauty, but the atmosphere was monstrous, so depressing. It was hard to breathe.

I met up with Harry again here and we decided to give our relationship another shot. That co-dependent relationship again, like a virus, wouldn't go away.

I began to think of my parents. I was deeply upset with the relationship I had with Mum, but as a wise old man once told me, I couldn't be responsible for her, but only to her. And Dad always seemed to gloss over things and never really dealt with anything. My half-sister, Melody, from Dad's first marriage, was much more my kind of person.

When I was eighteen I had spent a couple of years living with her and her two young children, and learned so much about relationships and functional families in her safe and loving home. When I was growing up, dinner conversation had always seemed to centre on my failures and how I could improve myself. After about six months with my sister, I began to eat with her family and break down this barrier. When I first moved in with her I would feel physically ill if I saw people hugging. Slowly I got used to seeing her hug and play with her children, and eventually became very affectionate myself. She was my role model for that period of my life, and had always been the only person who stood up for me with Dad.

I spent New Year's Eve in Spain, learning flamenco. The year had flown by in the breeze of what seemed like a second. Morocco next. Though only an hour from Spain by ferry, Morocco was very far from Europe.

- Chapter Eighteen -
A Narrow and Bumpy Escape

"All travel has its advantages.
If the passenger visits better countries,
he may learn to improve his own.
And if fortune carries him to worse,
he may learn to enjoy it ."
Samuel Johnson

When you don't trust your inner voice, events can open up which can be quite negative, even life threatening ...

I had been travelling all over the world and had amazing experiences. But nothing scared me more than my trip to Morocco when I was twenty four.

While Harry and I were on the ferry from Spain to Tangiers in Morocco, we met an American couple. After flicking through our copy of *The Lonely Planet,* we decided to all go to Marrakech together.

We arrived in Tangiers where I spent the day haggling for a silk carpet. I really did not intend to buy it, but found the bartering process so much fun that I stayed with it and eventually bought the carpet for $300 instead of the original price of $3500. 'Madam,' the shop owner had insisted as he took a lighter to the carpet, 'this is silk!'. The fact that the carpet did not catch on fire was apparently a big selling point. What a way to sell a carpet! I quickly folded it up into my backpack.

A guy we talked to on the platform at Tangiers told us not to go to Marrakech but to go to Fez instead. Apparently we would have a much better experience in Fez. But we were still intent on going to Marrakech.

The train from Tangiers to Marrakech took about two days. The four of us shared the six-berth carriage with two Moroccan guys. The train stopped occasionally, and we would hop out and buy sickly sweet mint tea.

We tried to make conversation with the Moroccan guys, but they spoke very little English. The American guy discovered they could speak Spanish, so they started to have a conversation in Spanish while we kept talking in English about taking a camel trip across the Sahara, other things we wanted to do, and how much money and time we had left for our trip. Even the Moroccan guys told us to go to Fez instead of Marrakech. Finally we decided to change our travel plans and go to Fez. This was our first mistake.

We left the train in Fez and started walking with the two Moroccan guys. Everything was whitewashed, making all the buildings look the same, it was almost like a maze. White temples, white houses, white walls – it was very confusing. We came to a small café, which was just a few tables and chairs on a brown dirt floor. There were some hessian bags hung casually around and a small camper stove in the back. We ordered mint tea and asked our two Moroccan guys where we could stay for the night. They said they would take us to the Medina and show us. We tried to get more details but they insisted on accompanying us to the Medina.

We started walking towards the gates of the Medina and once we were inside this small walled area of the city we each felt a little rise of panic. Without saying anything to each other, we all knew something was not right. It seemed that in all our youth and naiveté, we had been led right down the garden path. Rather than listening to our inner voices, we kept going deeper and deeper into the hole. Eventually we came to a house and when we asked what we were doing there, the guys said, 'Don't worry, you can stay with us'. This was their home, not the hotel they had promised they would find for us.

On the train, these two had said that they didn't know each other. When we got to the house, I asked the one who apparently did not live there where the bathroom was, and he pointed me in the right direction, so we knew that something was definitely very wrong. We knew we had made a mistake but didn't know what to do about it. We were still completely unaware of the full consequences of this mistake.

The two young men arranged a room for us to sleep in and shared a delicious meal of cumin chicken with us. We ate with our hands, as is the custom in Morocco. You must remember which hand is for what; one is for eating and one is for wiping.

The next day they took us on a car ride around Fez. We visited the markets, which were fabulous. We got into a discussion with a camel herder who wanted to buy me for the price of a few hundred camels. Harry appeared to be seriously considering the offer. Then we stayed another night at the house, becoming more and more nervous but not knowing what to do.

The next morning when we met them downstairs, the Moroccan guys suddenly started speaking in perfect English. I asked them why they had pretended not to speak English, and they said, 'English is boring.' Suddenly we realised that they had understood our conversation in regard to the money we carried.

One of the Moroccans asked each of us in turn to hand over the exact amount of money we had mentioned on the train, along with our passports. We were in shock. This was worse than bad. One of the American guys was thinking fast and said, 'We will give you half the money now and the other half when you take us back to the café.' The café was outside the Medina. This was really good thinking, and probably saved our lives.

We gave over half of our money and walked to the front door to go to the café. When we opened the door, waiting outside was the guy we had met on the train platform at Tangiers, who had told us that Fez was the place to go. You could have picked my jaw up off the floor. My eyes and heart froze simultaneously in fear. He was wearing black leather gloves and casually swinging his arms forwards and backwards. Every time his arms swung in front of his body, he clasped and unclasped his hands. Over and over he repeated this very menacing movement. His deep-set, dark eyes focused only forward. They were stone cold and heartless.

These men were obviously all connected and we were the wayward sheep in their sheep-herding expedition. It was a really slick operation, corralling unsuspecting tourists in the right direction to take their money. We had heard that the average wage in Morocco was five dollars a week. The thousands of dollars they would get from us would equate to years of work in the hot sun.

They took us back to the café, walking along making jokes in Moroccan while we were nearly wetting our pants. When we finally left the Medina and arrived at the café, we handed over the last of our money. They asked us for our passports, and in an attempt to buy time, the American guy said, 'Just a minute, let us look in our bags for them.' We all made a show of rummaging in our bags for the passports.

Then the strangest thing happened. We had not spoken to each other at all, knowing that the men could understand everything we said. We were all thinking that maybe these would be our last moments on earth.

A bread truck came around the corner, going really slow with the back door open. Without a word, we all grabbed our backpacks and ran for our lives, jumping into the back of the bread truck. We sat perched on squashed rolls and loaves while the unsuspecting driver just kept driving. A couple of kilometres out of town, he pulled over and asked, 'What are you doing?' We begged him to take us to the train station, which thankfully he did.

When we got to the station, we had no money for tickets to Tangiers or anywhere else. But we got on the train anyway and managed to get to Tangiers. How lucky we had been. We could have lost our passports and even our lives to those ruthless men.

As we sat on the train, our eyes the size of dinner plates, we kept asking each other the same question over and over. 'Why did you run?' 'Why did you run?' It was almost as if, in asking the question, maybe we would lose some of the anxiety that was so heavily burdening us. We never did answer that question, but we did accept the fact that it had probably saved our lives. I guess at some point, instinct really does kick in – the instinct to live.

This experience really showed me the importance of trusting your instincts, listening to that inner voice we all have but sometimes ignore. When you go blindly into situations bad things can happen, and not just in Morocco. Your gut feelings always guide you in the best direction.

In Tangiers we all contacted our families, trying to get money wired to us. The Americans planned to continue their travels and Harry was headed to Scandinavia, but I wanted to go home to Australia, where at least the con men seemed more civilised. Dad had seemed pretty sick when I spoke to him, so I used the last of the money in my bank account to go back to Cudgen to see him. I had been on the road for twenty two months.

- Chapter Nineteen -
Is Home Where The Heart Is?

"When there is a start to be made, don't step over! Start where you are."

Edgar Cayce

As soon as I arrived back at the house in Cudgen, I realised that Dad was not physically sick, he was just sick of not having control over me.

There was no celebration to welcome me home. I'd been away for nearly two years, but Dad acted as if he had seen me the previous weekend. He didn't seem interested in hearing about my trip or looking at my photos. We got straight back into our old habits, disagreeing over everything. I started to wish I had never come back.

Because I had rushed home to see Dad, he had said he would pay me back the price of my airfare. Something changed though, and the promise turned out to be empty.

I had come back to reality and responsibility with a jolt. It was time to start all over again, looking for work, cutting my hair, having a bath and getting out of my jeans. The taste of freedom I had was quickly vanishing.

I spent three days with Dad, but this was as long as I could stand. I hitchhiked to Sydney and stayed with friends, taking a waitressing job while I worked out what I wanted to do next in my career.

I was considering a job with Colgate-Palmolive, but the boss was dangerously handsome. To avoid sleeping with him, I took another job for much lower pay. Of course, he called to ask why I did not accept the job. I told a small white lie, saying I had a better offer. He promptly asked me out to dinner. Now there was no risk of sleeping with my boss, I said yes. I wasn't interested in a serious relationship, as I had too much to do, but I enjoyed his certainty and confidence; I love a strong man!

- Chapter Twenty -
A Soul Mate

*"The most important thing in life is to learn
how to give out love, and to let it come in."*

Morrie Schwartz

Soon I moved in with Mum at her place in Kings Cross. It was 1992 and I was twenty five, but I really didn't feel like taking advantage of the party lifestyle that was on my doorstep. I was more focused on building my career.

Mum convinced me to go out one evening; she just wanted me to have fun. I got dressed up in a combination of my clothes and Mum's, and went to a nondescript pub in the city for drinks with an ex boyfriend of mine, Shane. He introduced me to his two friends, Patrick and Christian. I was instantly attracted to Christian; he was tall, dark and wickedly handsome. Christian had a smile that could light up a dark scary night and a laugh that was so fabulous he could lead you home with it. He was smart, funny and witty to boot. His energy was just fabulous, totally irresistible.

At the end of the evening, Christian and Shane were arguing over who should put me into a cab. Patrick got between them and said, 'Let Christian put her into the cab, you were her boyfriend and now you are not.' So Christian flagged a cab and chatted to the cab driver. The next thing I knew he was kissing me. I felt myself melt into him. My skin softened and my mouth melted towards him as our passion drove us deeper into each other. I surrendered; the chemistry was too strong to fight.

My desire for him was so primal and so deep that I could not stay away from him. I was always waiting for the next touch, the next caress; I was like putty in his hands. Being with Christian was like diving into the most beautiful lake on a hot summer's day, letting the cool water wash over you, filling you with delight and love and a lust for life. I felt forever sexy and wanted and spoilt. What a fabulous experience.

He would call me up at a moment's notice and I could never refuse him. If I was at work, he would call and say 'Pack your bags, we are going away'. Then whisk me off for a weekend skiing or boating. It was so exciting, I felt so alive with the spontaneity of a partner who delighted in spoiling me in surprising ways.

He threw fabulous parties on balmy summer nights at his house in Neutral Bay. We would cater for around forty or fifty people, and Christian would walk around with a bottle in each hand. Guests would throw their heads back to have their drinks filled, straight into their mouths. We played and laughed, delighting in each other's company.

Christian had the most beautiful old Jag, as well as another old collector's car which started with a turning handle at the front. We would make out in the car, on his boat, in the house, anywhere. Once his flatmate walked into the room carrying two coffees for us, to be greeted by the sight of me astride Christian in a state of bliss. Somehow he managed to back out of the room and close the door without dropping the coffees onto the wooden floor. The look on his face was truly memorable. Christian and I broke into hysterics, enjoying the surprise.

I was introduced to Christian's parents at a dinner at their lovely home in Pymble. While we waited for them, Christian ravaged me on the couch. Of course they walked right in, and as I squirmed around attempting to assume a sitting position and fix my hair, Christian just stood up and introduced us as if nothing had happened.

We drank wine and ate sushi around the pool and I was grateful for the dimmed lights and the sound of the water, they hid my blushing and the swishing of my thoughts. I could barely make conversation, and silently begged him to take me home.

Christian was a beautiful lover and a beautiful friend. I think

I knew at the beginning that this was something special, but I didn't yet understand that I was programmed for sabotage and could not allow myself to be happy.

I had been seeing him for about two weeks when I said to my girlfriend, 'I think that's the guy I am going to marry.' At the same time he said to his best friend, 'I am going to marry this girl.' Our two friends concurred, this was serious, but I started to sabotage it straight away.

The downfall came when I realised how seriously rich he was. Just before Christmas in 1993, he showed me a small side table he had just bought. When he told me he had paid around $100,000 for it, I left him. I simply couldn't handle that much wealth.

My problem with money probably stemmed from my dad, who never spent quality time with me, he just spent money on me. So I grew up wanting time from my partners, not money. When I saw this huge display of wealth, I ran. I wish at the time I had understood why I reacted that way and could work through it. But I didn't find this piece of the puzzle for years. I was in love with Christian and we had the most amazing relationship. But what could I do? I only knew what I knew at the time.

So I left him, despite him begging me not to. I almost immediately regretted my decision and for the next four years tried to undo the damage and restart our relationship. But I had broken his heart and he would not have me back. He simply could not trust me anymore. I was the one who missed out, but I feel so blessed to have loved a kindred spirit on that level.

Now I understand the amazing choices that money gives, and the good it can do. Money is only energy and the fate of money is determined by the hands that hold it. It's such a pity that I didn't come to terms with that issue before the breaking point in our relationship. Hindsight is always so clever.

I returned to Canada for a holiday not long afterwards, and Harry met me at the airport. We spent a couple of weeks together, skiing with Cassie in Whistler. Late one afternoon, Harry and I caught a chairlift alone to the highest peak on the mountain. At the top of the mountain he got down on one knee and proposed. The snow was so slippery he almost slid away, it was so funny and yet romantic at the same time. He presented me with the most beautiful diamond ring, a large, classic clear solitaire.

I knew I couldn't marry him, I didn't love him and my heart was still battered from the break up with Christian. I told him I would think about it, but we both knew it wasn't going to happen. After a few weeks, I came back to Australia. He wanted me to take the ring with me, to see if I would change my mind, but I gave it back to him. He was devastated, but at last I had been clear with him and made a decision.

- Chapter Twenty-One -
The Loss Of Daniel

*"When you have come to the edge of all light
that you know and are about to drop off into
the darkness of the unknown, Faith is knowing
one of two things will happen:
There will be something solid to stand on
or you will be taught to fly."*

Patrick Overton

Occasionally in life, there are moments that are so significant that for the rest of your days, you will always remember where you were and what you were doing when they happened.

I was twenty seven, and I was visiting my sister Melody and her children at their home in Melbourne, as I often did when I was in Australia. Melody's phone rang, and as soon as she put it to her ear, I had a knowing feeling come over me, that my brother Daniel was dead. Melody said, 'Hi, Dad'. Then she turned to me and said that Daniel was dead. Those moments will always be chiselled into my memory, as vivid as can be. It was like the world had stopped.

Daniel had hanged himself on August 11th, 1994, but the phone call didn't come for a week afterwards, once he had already been cremated. I was so angry that Dad did not tell us earlier, and that the cremation had already happened. I tried to rationalise why Dad had done this; maybe it was the shock, maybe he had made the arrangements on the spot before he told anyone else.

Out of the whole family, I was the closest to Daniel. Melody was his half-sister, and they had never lived together, so her reaction was less extreme than mine.

The disbelief at Daniel's death swallowed me up until I was engulfed in the pain. I cried nonstop for the rest of the week, while everybody crept quietly around me. Melody and I barely spoke about the news.

I caught a coach from Melbourne to Sydney, crying all the way. 'Why, why why?' The question kept swirling around in my head, but of course there was no answer. Nothing seemed to make the pain go away. It hurt more every time I took a breath. My very being was contorted by it. People would see my pain and ask me if I was OK, but I would just burst into tears. For five years, his death flavoured every day of my life.

When I got to Sydney I had the awful task of letting Mum know that her son was dead. The only thoughts that kept burning through my brain were 'How do I tell my mum?', 'How do I tell her that her son has died?', 'When do I tell her?' There were no answers to these questions, but they continuously taunted my soul like cruel children in a school yard. There simply was no relief. What to do? What to do? Dad hadn't wanted to do it. So, I was left with the awful task on hand. It was going to kill me.

I took her to a little café with faded red roses on the tablecloths. After a few false starts, I finally got the words out, 'I've got to tell you something really bad. Daniel is dead'. Mum shot straight up, her back up against the wall. 'No, no, no, no', she wailed. Then she sat silently, dry eyed and still. She was in shock, and never fully recovered. A mother losing her child must be one of the hardest things a human can experience.

I moved into a flat in Neutral Bay with a friend from uni. Friends would come by to visit, but I was in a terrible state, and began to give away my possessions to anyone who would take them. Nothing I owned compared to my brother, and nothing could bring him back. Eventually I only had a mattress left on the floor.

A few weeks later there was a bashing on the door at 2 am. It was one of Daniel's best friends, demanding to know why I hadn't been at the memorial service. Memorial service? I hadn't heard anything about it. It turned out that my stepmother had arranged it, and had not invited me, my half-sister or Daniel's own mother. Shut out and away from the family, even at a time like that.

I had missed out on the closure that a funeral can bring, so I travelled to Margaret River in Western Australia, where he had died. Perhaps I could feel something of him there, and say goodbye.

Daniel had been the most beautiful child. He had incredible olive skin, bluer than blue eyes and incredibly blonde hair. In kindergarten the kids called him 'Curly Girly' and at school it was 'The Greek God'. He had always been shorter than me and I had spent most of my teenage years apologising to him for this, but finally when he turned sixteen he started to grow and eventually became a strapping six foot four. He was a highly accomplished chef and was engaged to be married when he took his life. He had shown no signs of depression; his suicide was totally unexpected.

Daniel was the one person who had loved me unconditionally as a child, and had been there for me no matter what. He had given me an inner light and strength which seemed to make life more solid. I went to a very dark place once he was gone, and my life would never be the same again.

The three months after my brother's death were complete hell as I tried to understand why such a promising life had been cut short. Daniel had suffered so much from Mum leaving the family, and feeling so unwanted afterwards. Maybe that's why he drank so much. When Mum came back into our lives, he was still very bitter. When he was sober, he would treat her terribly, but when he was drunk his feelings would show through, and his love and need for her would be obvious.

I couldn't cope with my high profile job as a project manager while I was coming to terms with what had happened, so I took a job as a waitress at Doyle's restaurant at Circular Quay in Sydney. But even that was a huge strain. I couldn't even talk about what had happened, and told people that my brother had died in a car accident if they asked.

- Chapter Twenty-Two -
Mindless Chores Equal Therapy

"The only cure for grief is action."
George Henry Lewes

During my years at university, I had met a bag lady sitting out the front of my local supermarket. I gave her a bottle of sherry, even though it probably wasn't what she ought to have, and sat down to chat. She told me she used to live in a nice house, with a nice husband and a nice son. One day, the son had gone out in the morning but he had never come back. An accident, they said, killed on the spot. 'Well, I wanted to die too,' the bag lady said to me. 'After all, my son needed me. But it is a sin to kill yourself. So I didn't. I just packed a few things and started walking. Done it ever since. Waiting for God to finally take me home.'

I had begun to see a psychiatrist to help me through my grief, and he wanted to hospitalise me. I knew that if I did this, it would be enough to make me give up altogether. There was still somewhere inside me a tiny little voice, willing me to survive, pushing me forward. And his way wasn't the way forward for me!

I bought another ticket to Canada.

Even after the disastrous marriage proposal, once I arrived back in Canada I went back to Harry. He had finally moved on and was no longer in love with me, but let me stay with him anyway.

I hung out at his house near Toronto for a year, working a little, but mostly just watching *The Jerry Springer Show*, *The Ricky Lake Show* and *Geraldo*. Watching other people's lives on TV, I could see that they were worse off than me, and it made my suffering feel that little bit smaller. Although

I wasn't aware of it at the time, my obsession with watching those talk shows probably trickled the idea into my head, that somehow, one day, I too could become unbroken, healed like the people on TV.

The other thing I did each and every day was to vacuum the carpet. There was a sense of achievement in this, a sense of accomplishment watching those lines appear, like a mower going over a lawn. I could clearly see where I had been and where I needed to go. Vacuuming became my therapy and a place that I felt safe. It was something normal that I could hold on to while everything else seemed to slip away. Once again, it was in the ordinary order of life that experiences became extraordinary.

I walked around the house in a towel and a t-shirt, contemplating my biggest daily decision: whether or not to have a shower. This was the extent of my ability to think. Anything else would have been overwhelming. If my decision was yes, I would consider moving onto the question of when. Often though, I would suffer anxiety over the decision I had made on showering. I wondered whether or not it was the right choice and would start to stress over it.

I no longer trusted myself with any decision making. Surely I would stuff that up too. I would begin to panic, then go back to vacuuming to make me feel safe. When you are pushed right to the edge of breaking, it's the little things that you hold onto. Like a drowning person clutches a small flotation device, small but life saving. I knew I had reached the threshold of what I could bear in pain.

When we are faced with a very difficult situation, we either handle it or we don't. If we can shed a positive light on it and move forward with that light, then we have the opportunity to not just handle it, but to grow and expand in ways that exceed our imagination.

I started to read self-help books. I was looking for stories of people who had felt what I felt and survived. I needed to find some hope in those books. During the next two years, I read over 400 self-help and psychology books.

One thing that became clear through all the reading, was that I had created my life's experiences, both good and bad, in order to fulfil my soul's purpose and destiny. I had lost both Frank and Daniel. Perhaps I had needed to lose my footing in this way twice in life, in order for me to understand the lesson fully.

After about eleven months of vacuuming, the cloud began to lift. Slowly the enormous burden I had been weighed down by had shifted and was somehow easier to carry. The demons that had been inside me started to quieten down, and I was able to think again.

- Chapter Twenty-Three -
The Way Forward

*"If you die today, what ideas, what dreams,
what abilities, what talents, what gifts
will die with you?"*

Les Brown

The truth, as they say, lies within. A seed already has its truth inside it when it is planted. It has a hidden agreement that under the right conditions it will flower and blossom into its own magnificent potential. We also have a truth, a purpose, a hidden agreement, and the experiences we have through our lives give us the opportunities to unlock it. It is nature's way and the way of universal energy.

As I came out of my fog of grief, I began to think about where to go from there. I had a degree in marketing, but had found the corporate sector didn't connect with me on a soul level. I was using my skills to do something I didn't really believe in, but I couldn't see what my options were.

So I began to search for a true purpose where I could make a difference in people's lives. I had no idea what this would be, so I tried everything I came across to see if I could uncover a secret yearning or passion that had been suffering from laryngitis up until now.

I tried my hand at jewellery making, woodwork and silver smithing. I shovelled horse manure, built wooden decks, installed spas, nannied and cleaned. It was all a big flop. The earrings didn't match, the deck was dangerous, and the table I made was wobbly (it couldn't even hold the weight of a teaspoon). It did not even look like a table, more of a stool moonlighting as a table. Perhaps this was a mirror of my life – was I a stool moonlighting as a person?

Or the other way around?

I was at a waitressing job when my friend invited me to a lecture at the Toronto School of Homoeopathic Medicine. 'Homeo who?' I said, but I went along anyway, rather than spend the weekend serving beer and fries.

The lecture was by Ray Edge, and I was mesmerised from the start. He seemed to be speaking the same way I thought. It was a clear and defining moment – I wanted to be a homeopath. Homeopaths study human behaviour, and prescribe remedies that mimic any condition that is causing a problem. The body reacts to that remedy by beginning to fight back. It therefore fights the problem, and in effect learns to heal itself.

And so began my quest for knowledge into the human condition, human behaviour, and the authentic reasons behind our behaviours, emotions and physical conditions.

I began a course of homeopathic treatment for my own issues, and was amazed at how they helped me to release the pain I was carrying. There was not a day that went by that I did not think about Daniel. This was a huge burden to carry, but homoeopathy offered me a place to breathe, to find the space to allow other thoughts into my head. Soon a day would pass and I would realise I hadn't thought about Daniel at all. Over time, that turned into two days and then three and then even weeks would go by. Eventually, I would watch whole anniversaries slip by and not even notice.

I also started therapy, which changed my core beliefs. I believe that everyone has an 'inner compass'. This is formed by the experiences you have had, and the values and beliefs you hold. It determines the direction you will take, and so if you wish to change direction, you must go back to these values and beliefs and change them first.

There is still sadness, for while time heals, it does not take away the pain completely. It is still there, and like an old sore, if you prod it and poke it enough it will weep and eventually bleed. In life though, it is important to have extreme experiences to show you what you are capable of. It would be tragic to die with your song still inside you.

It is up to you to play your song and enjoy the music that it makes. You are a living, harmonic, artistic creation of music that has not yet been fully written. The only way your song will ever be written into a memorable, significant piece, will be if you try out all the instruments, test their strength, sound, range and timbre. All the instruments inside you need to be tested in different ways. It is only by this process that you will find the sweetness of your soul. How you combine these instruments will be directly related to your beliefs, attitudes and ability to change and grow.

One of the realisations I gained from my brother's death, was that I was not ever going to waste any opportunity that came my way. I was compelled to help others, to make a difference. Equipped with the experience of getting through such depth of pain, I could no longer stand by and watch others suffer. I made a commitment to live for both Daniel and myself, now that he was gone and I was the eldest child in the family. Daniel's death gave me the opportunity to find meaning in my own life, and I realised how important it is to live every moment.

I stopped worrying that someone might think I was too fat, too tall, too this or too that. I stopped worrying completely about what other people thought. That was truly liberating. As long as I was not hurting anyone else, I just did my thing, with love and kindness. I can now share my story, warts and all, because I am no longer afraid to be judged. We are judged every minute of the day anyway. It's just that I stopped taking it personally.

All that time and money on counselling and self development set me up so very well, for myself and ultimately for my clients. The most important money you will ever spend, is the money that you spend on the six inches of real estate between your ears. There is nothing more valuable.

I had visa issues and had to return to Australia, so I put the homeopathic training on hold for a while. Eventually I was able to return, once I received my 'landed' status, which allowed me to work and study. I got a job back in Whistler and studied homeopathy at the Vancouver

Homeopathic Academy for four years, then went on to do a Masters in Homeopathy with Lou Klein in Seattle. My dad, the doctor, said it was all a waste of time.

- Chapter Twenty-Four -
The Family Grows

*"Courage is the first of the human qualities because
it is the quality that guarantees all the others."*

Sir Winston Churchill

Preparing for my first trip back to Canada, Mum was distraught that I was leaving, not knowing if I was coming back or not. I told her that I only planned to go for five weeks, but it didn't seem to make any difference to her. I guess all those years of not having her children around meant that she held on tightly to any time that she could have with us. She knew me well though; I was back and forth between Canada and Australia for over a decade after this.

We had an enormous argument the night before I left and Mum threw everything I owned into the hallway of our tiny place at Kings Cross. Friends helped me get all my gear into garbage bags and over to their house in Neutral Bay, and with only a few hours until my early morning flight, we frantically dug through the garbage bags to find my traveller's cheques, passport and tickets. By about 6 am we'd found it all, but I left a shocking mess in my friend's garage as I raced to Sydney airport. Later, on the plane, I went to tidy myself up and noticed in the bathroom mirror a belt buckle shape clearly imprinted on my neck, a legacy from the fight with Mum. I guess she would be coming with me on the journey after all.

When I got back from Canada five weeks later, I finally had a chance to clean out my gear from my friend's garage, and came across a Louis Vuitton bag that Mum had lost during our argument. As she threw everything into the hallway, she had begun to freak out, looking frantically for her Louis Vuitton bag which had got mixed up in all the mess. And now here it was, in amongst all my jumbled possessions.

I opened the designer bag to find a bundle of letters written in German – Mum is half German and half Norwegian. No wonder she was so worried about losing the bag. I was curious about what was in the letters, having grown up in a family of secrets. I am sure that is why my life has been an open slather, with nothing to hide. I asked a German friend to help me translate them, and spent an afternoon listening to my friend read out the letters one after the other.

The letters were from my mother's parents. When I was about eight years old, my grandfather had come to see me at a ballet performance, but that is the only contact I had ever had with my grandparents. Although they lived in Germany, I wanted to reconnect with them and establish some sort of relationship.

I started writing to them, and after the third letter I received a tape in return. It was so special to hear their voices in halting English as they told me about their lives. They mentioned that they were going to have Christmas dinner with my brother.

I just could not fathom that – I had another brother? Coming so soon after Daniel's suicide, it was hard to comprehend that another brother had appeared from nowhere. I didn't want this new brother, I wanted Daniel back, the brother I had known all my life and loved so much.

Apparently, in the early years of Dad's first marriage, he had taken a trip to Europe, leaving his wife and two children behind. While in Paris, he went on a date with another woman to one of those cabaret shows where the girls wear nothing more than feathers. At the show he met my mum for the first time. She was also on a date with someone else.

By the end of the night, Mum and Dad were a couple. Who knew what happened to their unfortunate dates! Dad proposed to Mum within 24 hours. It appeared to be only a minor technicality that he was already married. My parents then bought a VW bug and travelled around Europe for eight weeks. At the time, Mum was around nineteen years old, and four months pregnant with another man's child. When Dad returned to his wife and kids in Australia, he asked my mum to come out and be with him. However he would not allow her to bring the child.

So Mum adopted out her first son, Sydney. His name is now Tom. I think this was Mum's first deep wound, the beginning of a pattern of losing the children she adored and cherished.

When she moved to Sydney, Australia, Dad put her in a unit in Rockdale and happily went between his wife and my mum. After a while, Mum had enough of that arrangement and decided to get herself a boyfriend. Dad was so furious that he left his wife and two kids and moved in with my mum. They went on to have three kids, Daniel, myself and Jarrod, and eventually Dad got divorced from his first wife and finally married my mum.

Once I had calmed down about finding out about this brother, I wanted to bring him closer into our family. The need to have family, any sort of family, was so important to me. Coming from such a fractured background meant I was constantly trying to collect people and look after them, drawing them in to me in an attempt to heal that space inside me. I found it very hard to change schools as a child, and leave behind friends I had made. My favourite show was *The Waltons,* and the idea of having a brood of happy children around me like a 'Waltons' family became a lifelong dream.

After about a year of writing to each other we were ready to meet, and Tom came out to Australia. I hoped that it would be cathartic for Mum also, seeing her first-born again. Tom was very handsome; I think his dad must have been Spanish. He had Mum's sense of class and style. Unfortunately this part of her genes seemed to skip over me entirely!

- Chapter Twenty-Five -
A Spiritual Awakening

"This is my simple religion.
There is no need for temples;
no need for complicated philosophy.
Our own brain, our own heart is our temple;
the philosophy is kindness."

The 14th Dalai Lama

As a child, I knew beyond a doubt that God existed. I covered a bottle with aluminium foil and put lovely flowers in it, then put it out in the garden as a gift for God.

As I got older, I was still convinced there was a universal energy and I was an instrument of the will of some divine being. But I began to wonder who this God was, how much power God had and how this all came about.

As part of this slow awakening, I began to study different religions of the world. I looked into Buddhism, Zen, Catholicism, Hinduism and the Quakers. There was much to learn, and lots of great stories.

Some of the religions I studied had a definite sense of right and wrong. There was a black and white nature to them. I didn't think life was black and white, at least my life certainly wasn't. Life to me was shades of grey.

I began to lean more towards the Eastern religions, kinder religions that were gentler, more embracing. I liked the idea that you did not have to feel guilty for the choices you made, they were just part of the journey. These religions actually embraced other points of view as part of their all inclusive and loving philosophy.

In particular, I was drawn towards Buddhism and its three main philosophies: unconditional love, understanding, and compassion.

It seemed to me that while the Ten Commandments had their place and it was good to have rules to live by, they didn't apply to every situation. However, compassion, understanding, love, and a willingness to look at things from other people's points of view, created more harmony and peace in the world.

To get into a discussion of 'good' or 'bad' becomes too complicated, as it comes down to personal judgements. If you accept your life without any judgement, and simply believe that the opportunity to experience life, with the good, the bad and the ugly IS the gift, then you start to see new possibilities for yourself and the way you live.

I also began to understand that what you believe creates the reality you experience. If you think it's impossible to have any money, then you won't have any money. If you think it's impossible to have any love, then you won't have any love, and so on.

Even as you change, progress and develop, you are still affected by your residual thoughts. The thoughts and beliefs that you had six months ago, have created the reality that is the life you now lead. For things to change, first you must change your ideas, values and beliefs about your life. Then your reality will begin to change to reflect these new beliefs.

Although I was not a Buddhist, I wanted to explore these philosophies further, so when I was thirty I attended a Vipassana retreat in the Blue Mountains, west of Sydney. One of the fundamentals of Buddhism is meditation, which was the basis of this retreat. I never do anything by halves, it's all or nothing with me, so I jumped right in at the deep end with a ten day silent retreat. There was no talking, no looking at anyone, just meditating and eating greens and rice in silence. It just about killed me.

The daily program started at four in the morning and went on until ten at night. There were group meditations, individual meditations, lectures and walks. But the most powerful part for me was the sensory deprivation. I came very, very close to myself and it was an uncomfortable place to be.

I had no idea how to be silent. The isolation was extreme. People around me reacted to it in different ways: crying, screaming or laughing. Being forced to be by yourself with no outside stimulation is a near impossible feat for many people, including me.

The first minute of silent meditation seemed like years. I managed to sit through that first minute, then another minute. I began to contemplate that there were nine days and tens of thousands of minutes to go. All that time stretching out in silence, so deafening I could hardly stand it. How would I ever make it through?

I began to worry that the minutes would never end and I would be completely swallowed up in them. I would go completely crazy; there was just way too much empty time. Nothing and then nothing on top of nothingness until I couldn't make sense of the time I was doing this for. I might begin stacking blocks of nothing on top of each other, an endless game of Lego where even making the pieces reach the sky would do nothing to shift my discomfort at more nothing.

I was not going to make it, surely I was not. What was the point again? I started to panic as I sensed I was losing control. I wasn't the captain of the ship any more. There was a battle between what my soul wanted and what my ego wanted. Silent meditation was a place where the volume of my soul was turned up, and the ego took a back seat.

I started to get a true appreciation of time and the fact that it does not just run out. I made it run out, not least by my desire to always be busy. I started to have an inkling that maybe there was a greater purpose to my life.

But it was a fight, it was a process. It may not be a fight for everyone, but it is always a process, to find and focus on the soul and give it some space to grow. It was like wandering through acres of thick dense forest, looking for a tiny white flower. Walking for hours and hours through the trees, hungry and thirsty and beginning to become delirious. Forgetting what you are looking for, stumbling towards the deep oblivion of unconsciousness. Then, when you least expect it, the tiny white flower appears, just as your soul appears in the silence.

And suddenly there you are, with yourself. In fact you never left, you just became too busy to look. After all, your greatest relationship is with yourself, so why not get comfortable and start to go through the layers until you find your source – your eternal light? You always carry it within, you may have simply forgotten it is there. You may be surprised to find that you are your own best friend.

We cover up our true selves with shopping, working, partners, kids, friends, groceries, cleaning, playing, fun, holidays, banking – the minutiae of daily life. Everything is rushed and scattered, without honouring the gift of life and the time that we have. We eat on the go, do the dishes, put on the laundry, get the kids off to school, go to work and then home, dinner, TV and off to sleep. One day rolls into another and we do it all over again. Our lives fly by, unconscious of self, because there is no self in our day-to-day activities. We do not allow ourselves the experience of being conscious in each and every moment.

If we truly saw life as a gift, something to be treasured, we would surely live differently. If you were the only person on the planet to have a life, the only one who was going to have the opportunity of this experience, you would certainly not waste a second. You would plan out all the amazing things you wanted to do. You would embrace learning as you watched your understanding of everything in your world expand. Your consciousness, love, and light, would expand and so would your bliss and happiness. Consider: is this how you are living your life right now?

I was very lucky to have the opportunity to do a silent meditation retreat. I must admit it hardly seemed lucky at the time. In the middle of the retreat, I had a bit of a breakdown from all the silence, and didn't think I would make it through. I did make it, however by the end of the retreat I felt I had been away from society for at least ten years.

As I got into my car to drive home, I turned the radio on so I could listen to something, anything. An advert came on for two-minute noodles. Suddenly I felt that the noodles were right there in the car with me. I could feel the container, smell the noodles, and taste them. I was so involved in that advert, so present in it. Something had changed.

As I got back into my life, I began to notice that when I was interacting with other people, I now felt fully present. I was free of distractions and could fill up on what the other person was sharing. My thoughts were not absorbed by outside influences, like the clothes they were wearing, the way they wore their hair, the other appointments I had that day, the smell in the air. I was open and empty to receive that person.

I became able to listen without my mind wandering off in different directions. I could empty myself of judgment and hold a space of loving kindness for this soul in front of me. I could see the child in each adult, and I became so much more compassionate and loving of the human condition and our suffering. I began to see how I could help people to shine, and the ripple effect that this would have on the world around me.

I never went to another meditation retreat. It was much too hard. However, it certainly did have a lasting effect on my ability to be present and focused and totally there with my clients. I remained more aware of my purpose and the love that I have to share. Fifteen years later, I would say fifty percent of that ability still remains. To help keep this open inside myself, I began to meditate for about fifteen minutes a day, at least four times a week.

Learning how to deepen my interactions with people through meditation has been a wonderful gift and support, and has helped to heal the scars of the loss of my brother and being excommunicated from my family. It is a great way to focus daily on staying true to yourself.

To further my learning about Buddhism and Eastern philosophy, I went on to volunteer for the Dalai Lama when he visited Australia the same year. I was fortunate enough to sit in on some of his speeches in Sydney and to be part of his tour. The Dalai Lama is so unconditionally loving and giving, and he is so very present in the moment. He is an endearing cross between an old man and a very silly boy. His speeches are full of wisdom as well as giggly laughter. There is much to be said for that kind of life: giving, present, nurturing, wise, and very silly.

I also discovered *The Tibetan Book of Living and Dying* by Sogyal Rinpoche. This is a great book for those wanting an understanding of the Buddhist philosophy of death and dying. I first read this book when my brother committed suicide and I was trying to understand life and death. At that time it took me about three years to read it. Ten years later, I picked it up again, and this time I read it in two weeks. There are times when we are ready for life's lessons, and times when we are not.

When you awaken your life to the possibility of a soulful existence, then you have true joy, true meaning and a true 'life'. That's when you are living the dream.

- Chapter Twenty-Six -
Surviving India

"Opportunities to find deeper powers within ourselves come when life seems most challenging."
Joseph Campbell

When I was thirty two, I travelled to India for six months to study homeopathy. There, I was lucky enough to be taught by some of the most famous homoeopaths in the world. It was truly an enriching experience, as well as a huge eye-opener.

Learning about homeopathy gave me an understanding of the human condition and the way we each so uniquely experience our lives. It was so much more than a study in natural therapies – it was a way to live, a way to think and a way to breathe. It resonated with me and would become one of my first milestones in true liberation and just 'being'. I lapped up the training course like a kitten with a plate of milk.

After the study had ended, I decided to travel around India for a while, which was a singular and incredible experience. There was an unfathomable chasm between the beauty of the landscape and the heartbreaking existence of many of the people living in it. I saw people living on the streets in incredible poverty, being intentionally mutilated to earn money as beggars. The children affected me the most, with those old eyes, so full of pain.

I went from Mumbai through the state of Gujarat to a tiny little town called Bhuj. Here I found nothing but dust, Brahmin cattle and aimlessly wandering people. Everything seemed to be different shades of brown, and the taste of dust was always in my mouth. My face felt grimy and my hair was brittle, dry and gritty. It was as if I had had the life sucked right out of me and all that was left was a parched paper bag.

This area of India was renowned for its handicraft, and the beautiful block printed fabrics in bold colours were everywhere, pinned to the earth with rocks on their corners. They created an amazing multicoloured carpet, flapping in the wind as they dried on the dusty earth.

The string-bean locals would comment that I looked 'bored' today, but I had looked 'at ease' yesterday. I could not believe that they had the time to study me, a stranger to their village. It was a little bizarre to me to be surrounded by people who seemed to be able to read my mind; they were so in tune with the world around them.

After another day in the fields, mesmerised by the colourful fabric canvas covering the earth, I had returned to Bhuj with yet another tummy bug. I was one of the many travellers who did not have the cast-iron stomach needed to withstand India's constant onslaught of germs and disease.

As I lay in my bed at the guest house feeling sorry for myself, I heard a voice say to me to 'leave, leave now'. I ignored it, concentrating instead on the more urgent needs of managing the pain in my stomach and endless trips to the bathroom. A little while later I heard it again, 'Leave, leave now'. The voice was stronger this time. Eventually, a third time, the voice boomed loud and clear, as if it would burst right through the roof. 'Leave, leave now!' it yelled at me. I decided that maybe I should leave.

I believed that everything had a reason and my spirit guides were obviously trying to tell me something important. As sick as I was, I forced myself off the bed and began to pack my things, worrying about leaving the security of the guesthouse bathroom in my delicate condition.

One of the unwritten rules of travelling in India, is that a single woman should never travel alone at night. The Brahman man who owned the youth hostel was standing downstairs, and was astonished when I asked him to drive me to the train station. He was very concerned for my safety, a sick woman travelling alone at night, but I told him that I must go. I begged him to drive me, as I was so ill I could not walk far.

The train station was crowded, as Indian train stations always are. At any time of the day or night in India, there are always throngs of people trying to get onto any available train or bus. It was a similar scene to leaving the stadium after a major event, but this mayhem was played out day in, day out. Sometimes the wait for a ticket could take days. Of course this night, everything I tried to board was fully booked.

Luckily, my driver noticed a friend of his who owned a bus. He asked if I could fit on the bus, which was headed to Rajasthan. The bus owner politely offered for me to board the bus and choose a seat. I nearly giggled at the idea of having my own seat. I had travelled on enough Indian buses to know that people sat in the aisles on upturned plastic and metal buckets, hung out of windows, and even sat on the roof with ropes slung through rusty openings to hold their belongings. But he asked a man to stand up and I sat down in amazement on my very own seat. Then the fun began.

Indian buses are incredible. They swerve all over the road while honking their horns constantly, and now and again stop so the passengers can get out and be sick on the side of the road. How they manage to keep driving in the state they are in is a miracle. This bus was so old that it did not appear to have anything holding the front end onto the rear of the bus, and I kept waiting for it to detach completely whenever we pulled away from a stop. The other passengers did not even seem to notice.

The Indians appear to find some calm in the knowledge that their lives are hanging in the balance every day, while we westerners refuse to accept the cycle of life and somehow make believe we are invincible. We fill our lives full of material things and forget the true gift that life gives us. Nowhere in the world is this fact more obvious than in India.

Despite the odds, eight hours and about eight flat tyres later we arrived in Jaiselmere, Rajasthan. As we alighted from the bus, there was a strange metallic smell in the air and then, without warning, a massive earthquake hit us.

I was literally surfing on the ground, trying to stay upright. I prayed for the ground not to open up and swallow me. For some reason, I wasn't worried about the buildings falling down around me, only about being swallowed up.

It seemed like about two hours, but it was probably only two minutes, before the earthquake stopped. Immediately, people began running around screaming and panicking. It was complete mayhem.

There seemed to be nothing else to do, so I found a youth hostel and asked for a room. When I went upstairs, I saw that the roof had collapsed into the room. My timing had been perfect. If I had arrived in Jaiselmere on the bus ten or twenty minutes earlier and gone to the hostel, I would have been history. I went back out into the street and found a tiny eating-place with a couple of tables and chairs and a small television in the corner.

The television was showing a news flash about Bhuj, the town I had just come from in Gujarat. It had just been completely flattened by the earthquake. An estimated 16,000 people had died. I had been told three times to leave, and my guides had been right! I was in shock.

I went on a camel safari into the desert for the next two days, to create some quiet space and try to process what had just happened. I reflected that there must have been a reason why my life was spared. I had to go back to help those who hadn't been so lucky.

My first day back in Bhuj was like being in a war zone. There were military personnel, dead bodies and looting all around. The smell of death was so strong in the air. Dogs were running around with what looked like human remains in their mouths. Was this the set of a bad movie? I felt sick. Like the dogs, I had bitten off more than I could chew.

I didn't have the skills or the constitution to help on the front-line, so I joined a group packing emergency boxes with blankets, saline solution and medical supplies. I packed boxes for about eighteen hours a day, and at the end of the week, I broke down. I boarded a bus in tears, not knowing or caring where I was going. I think it was Nepal. Three months later, half my hair fell out from the after effects of the shock. It never completely grew back.

The experience of being told to leave Bhuj, and then so many people dying there and the town being wiped out, solidified my belief in universal energy. You may call it God or something else, but I believe these are just names for the same thing: a universal spiritual being or entity.

After this experience I had complete faith in my guides. If I am still, and listen, I can feel that I am guided all the time. Meditation was the key that helped my mind be quiet enough to hear my soul, my genuine self. When you start having a connection to this universal love, this spiritual energy, you can start to heal your own soul and hear it resonate with spiritual energy. It is the most beautiful, beautiful thing to experience.

After this experience, I did not have to try to *be* love each and every day, I just was. I gained faith in my path, which was to help as many people as possible. And I was able to begin moving forward on that path, confident that I was taking the right steps even when I didn't know why. I began to understand that I was a spiritual being in an emotional body moving towards the light and agreeing to fulfil my destiny, to fulfil my true purpose. Mum always said that I was 'totally out to lunch', but I knew it was just that I was fully guided by my spirits.

- Chapter Twenty-Seven -
Making Business Sense

*"All labour that uplifts humanity has dignity
and importance and should be undertaken
with painstaking excellence."*

Martin Luther King, Jr.

I was constantly drawn back to Canada, and spent sixteen years there on and off. Each time I visited, I wasn't able to stay as long as I wanted, due to limitations on my visa, so I always left the country wanting more.

I returned to Canada after my trip to India with my understanding of homoeopathy truly deepened. My experience of life itself was so much more intense, and the practice of homeopathy from this perspective was one of observing miracles each and every day. I wanted to help others with what I had learnt.

Life so far, had told me I was a winner. I had won awards as an athlete, then a horse rider, beach girl, business student and employee. It all came very easily to me. So, at thirty two, I thought I could do anything and be successful. I may have been wrapped up in ego. I may have been way too confident. I identified myself as successful; that was my experience and that was also my mistake.

I went to the Community Futures Department and applied for funding to start my own business, working from home as a homeopath. The lady who interviewed me believed in what I was doing, saw that I had degrees in business and marketing, and I got the funding.

This funding lasted a year while I began my homeopathic business from home. It was a great start for me, and allowed me to set up the business properly without stressing too much about the income.

After the funding ran out, I got talking to the same lady at Community Futures Department again. As she asked about my plans, it became clear that we both would love to have a wellness retreat. We decided then and there to go into business together.

I was very naïve and didn't even think of getting a business agreement or a partnership agreement. We just went forward on a wing and a prayer. I trusted that our business would work, simply because my life so far had shown me that I could achieve whatever I wanted.

Within a few weeks, we had found a building that would be perfect for our spa, and made plans for a fairly major renovation to get it ready. My business partner decided that this would be a good time to take a long holiday to Hawaii. This should have been a red flag to me, but I trusted that she would help out soon and everything would be fine.

I forgot that our current behaviour is what creates our life, not our potential. Potential remains just that, potential, until your behaviour changes. There is no point hoping for a different outcome based on the fact that you know the person has the potential to do things differently. Nothing will change unless that person chooses to change their behaviour, and takes action to do so.

An amazing team of about a dozen helpers gathered to work on the renovation, which was a major refit of the interior of the building. We chiselled 1300 square feet of laminate tiles off the floors by hand, a sea of white laminate slowly and painfully disappearing. I had no money for wages, so paid the team with beer and pizza. It was a huge effort, but so rewarding as we watched an uninhabitable building that stank of urine become a beautiful and welcoming place where people could feel relaxed.

The spa had an Eastern feel, with no white in it at all. There were tiny little pieces of mirror on the ceilings so it looked like a starry night. The treatment rooms were all different Chakra colours, bold and strong in purple, red, orange and blue. Each treatment room had floating wooden floors and either a statue or a picture of a Buddha. Other rooms had floors that were hand pressed with little pebbles, starfish and seashells. A very talented designer helped us to plan it, and as it came together someone said we should have put it on one of those renovation shows.

The spa was in a ski resort. People would come straight off the slopes in the afternoon to see us for a treatment. I did homeopathy and medical intuitive readings, and we also offered waxing, facials, manicures, pedicures and more. We had an amazing array of customers from all walks of life and no two days were the same.

My best work within the homeopathic world was always with people who were grief stricken, depressed or suicidal, because I was comfortable going to those places of pain to help my clients. These were emotions I had felt so often that they did not frighten me. I also had great success helping clients with anxiety, stress and depression, conditions that affect the mind and in turn affect the body.

I saw a little boy, only two years old, who had been on around 25 antibiotic treatments in his short life. His growth had been stunted and his parents were at their wits' end. I spent some time with him and gave him a remedy. In the following eight years he didn't need antibiotic treatment again, and caught up to his peers in height.

Another client came to me with severe alopecia, a kind of hair loss. For ten years she had tried to find a solution, with no success. Eventually she had become anxious and depressed. I gave her a remedy and a few months later she called, almost giggling on the phone, to tell me that her hair was growing at a rapid rate.

It can be difficult to understand the power of homeopathic treatments. It is truly an amazing medicine. It works with and for the body, and more specifically, with the mind and not against it.

A lady I treated had cervical cancer and had developed severe anxiety and eczema due to her illness. She could not drive a car because she was afraid that if she broke down, there would be no one to help her. Her children were not allowed on sleepovers with friends, in case something happened to them. She was a qualified Heli ski instructor but was no longer able to go up in the helicopter in case she had an anxiety attack. Her life had really stalled, but after homeopathic treatment, things began to change for her. Her skin cleared, she was able to drive a car, her children were allowed more freedom and she restarted her career as a Heli ski instructor. She even won a skiing competition. It was such a joy to see her move back towards a life worth living. I intentionally avoid using the 'normal' tag to describe her life; after all, what is normal?

One of the things that kept me in the health and wellness industry was the way it helped people on so many levels. In the corporate world, I had found that feelings didn't come into play at all. It was more about achieving targets, reaching Key Performance Indicators, and making reports. But in this industry, success was measured very differently.

One day a mechanic with long greasy hair and stained clothes came to see me. He was 50 pounds overweight and had an attitude of, 'Why am I here? I can give you half an hour, then I'm outta here'. I told him that I would try to get him an answer in half an hour. I found a remedy for him, Aurum 200c, even though he said he couldn't pay me, because, 'That's just the way it is'. He told me he was living on macaroni and cheese every night and maybe he would come back in six weeks, maybe he wouldn't.

Six weeks later he called to say he was feeling a little better and would contact me again soon. In another six weeks, he called again and told me he was getting a haircut. I could feel that something was definitely changing in him. I was so excited that he was starting to take some care with his appearance. A few weeks later, he told me he was riding a bike to work, so he could get a little fitter. Next, he told me he wanted to change his diet as macaroni and cheese had lost its appeal. I was really happy for him and the changes he had made. It all started with a homeopathic remedy.

It moves me when someone claws their life back, and begins to believe that the sun will shine tomorrow and that they have a life worth living. Seeing someone find joy and happiness is so rewarding.

About a year later, I was standing in line in a bank and a good looking, well dressed man came up to me and said, 'Hello, I'll bet you don't remember me.' I stared at him and no, I did not recognise this man. He grinned at me 'It's me, the mechanic you saw about a year ago!' I was stunned. He had lost 50 pounds, was clean-shaven and had shiny, neatly cut hair. He looked fifteen years younger! For the rest of the day, I cried whenever I thought of the happiness I could see in this man. It was humbling to be able to be a part of such a drastic change in someone's life.

Many months later, he called just as I was leaving the office to return the vehicle I had leased. I had decided that I could not really afford it, and when the mechanic asked what I was going to drive I said I did not need a car. He had two vehicles and offered me one, but I refused. Nevertheless, the next day I found not one but two vehicles in my driveway to choose from. I was overwhelmed by his kindness. I ended up driving his cool red and black Jimmy truck for nearly two years. What generosity!

We made 80% of our income at the spa in the sixteen weeks of the ski season. After that, it was a matter of surviving until the next ski season. It was a highly competitive and seasonal business. Even with the best weather and economic conditions, it presented quite a challenge.

Having a seasonal business meant we were constantly hiring. I was lucky to spend a day with a guy who worked closely with Bill Gates. He gave me some invaluable tips on hiring staff that I have carried with me to this day. I was so lucky to get the right advice at the right time.

I ended up doing thousands of job interviews, as we would employ a team of around thirty five people for the ski season, and then go down to just eight or ten staff for the rest of the year. At the beginning of the next season, we would be hiring again.

The team consisted of some very interesting and creative therapists, including massage therapists, a life coach, pilates and yoga instructors and an Ayurvedic doctor who had been trained by Deepak Chopra. Sometimes, a therapist would show up and say, 'I can't do this massage because the moon is at the wrong angle tonight', and I would say, 'Just get in there and rub some body'. Once a therapist had a melt down and walked out, leaving a client lying in the treatment room with wax still on her legs. That was an interesting one to fix in a hurry! It has always fascinated me the way people behave, and I built up such a wealth of experience in how to manage different personalities.

Once a twenty-one-year-old single mum came to me looking for work. We went through the usual interview process and I really liked her, but at the end of the interview she looked at me and said, 'You probably won't hire me because I am a single mum.' I said, 'I probably will hire you for that exact reason. As a single mum you would have to be so responsible to juggle your work and your child, that's exactly why you will get the job.' She was one of the best employees we ever had. She was so dedicated. Sometimes your lot in life will determine the quality of the function you perform.

Some people stop putting in such a big effort once they are comfortable and earning a good income. A single mum with a baby understands the opportunity she has been given, and I always like to reach out and help those who want to help themselves.

The clients also provided endless entertainment and opportunities for me to learn more about human nature. A lady came in wearing a mink coat worth about $20,000. We had tiny little tea lights everywhere for atmosphere, and after a few minutes the room was filled with the smell of burnt mink. I went pale thinking of the lawsuit that would certainly follow. But as the flames licked at her coat, the lady simply looked at me, smiled and said, 'It doesn't matter, just gives me an excuse to get a new one'. You could have knocked me over with a feather.

During Gay Ski Week, a customer took a shine to one of our therapists. As the therapist took the client into the therapy room, his last words were, 'If you hear screaming, come and get me!'

Of course, there were always those clients who, no matter how clearly you explained that they needed to get under the sheet for their treatment, would be sitting there bright and happy in their birthday suit ready to surprise the therapist. One lady from Japan was seen running naked through the spa saying she had lost her towel. I was sure she had lost more than just her towel, and I had to corner her in the Vichy shower room until I could find a robe and her therapist.

We were always fully booked for big occasions. One very fancy-looking lady would not take no for an answer, and demanded that she have her eyebrow wax NOW. She didn't care that all the rooms were full, and the only way I could appease her was to bring a therapist to the reception area and do it while she stood there. I bent so many rules and learned so many great things, such as, 'It is better to ask for forgiveness than to ask for permission'. I love that one!

- Chapter Twenty-Eight -
More Work Than Money

"All is well.
Everything is working out for my highest good
And out of this experience, only good will come,
and I am safe."

Louise Hay

When we started the spa, my business partner and I went in with equal investments. I had a good credit rating, and had successfully received funding for my home-based business. However, I couldn't get any funding to set up the spa, so I applied for ten credit cards at the same time. Within a couple of weeks, I had $100,000 credit. I thought it was a great way to raise the money I needed, but the interest on those cards was phenomenal. I think I paid well over $60,000 in interest alone.

The spa business was never really financially successful. We got audited three times and nearly went broke eight times. To our credit, the business did last ten years. In the first year or two, we were making a half million dollars per annum, but by the end we were doing only around $200,000.

When we opened our business, there were only four spas in town, so we had quite a huge share of the market. By year ten, there were 22 spas, so our share of the market had just kept falling. There were also other negative factors, such as 9/11, then the insurance prices tripling, then a couple of seasons where we had no snow at all.

I had five businesses before this, yet this one was my only partnership that actually had retail locations. We had built the business up pretty fast and within eighteen months had renovated again to move the office upstairs, then expanded over the road to a more prestigious location. We thought this would be a great answer to ever dwindling sales and a presence that was all but invisible with the competition in our town. Our location was hidden – downstairs and in the basement. Mind you, some of the most successful spas in the world are basement spas, but ours wasn't one of them.

But our biggest problem was our toxic business partnership. We never got that together. We could never agree on anything. If she wanted to do one thing, I wanted to do another. Our egos were constantly battling, constantly at war. We did try to make it work. We employed a business coach, who pronounced us un-coachable. Then we employed a life coach, who couldn't do much for us either. After this, we engaged a mediator for around eighteen months. After five minutes at those meetings we would be at each other's throats. I tended to attract bullies; I guess this was in order to learn how to deal with them. I must have been a slow learner, I kept doing it again and again!

More and more money was sunk into this sinking ship and instead of abandoning it, we were going down with it in the mistaken belief that somehow we could raise it and bring it back to life. We were quite visionary in what we wanted to do, and hoped one day to build a school to teach people how to become spa technicians.

I was desperate to find a way to pay the staff and keep this sinking ship afloat. I could not stop; could not allow myself to admit that it had failed. In my desire for change, I had watched the movie, *The Secret,* 41 times. I could recite the lines on demand. One morning I woke up saying the words of Michael Beckwith, 'And out of nowhere, from nothing, a way will be found'.

Just after this, a very wealthy local man showed up at my doorstep and asked how things were going. I said 'pretty terrible' and he asked me what I needed and why. I said, 'I have to make the payroll today and I am $15,000 short'. Incredible as it may seem, he simply pulled out a chequebook and wrote a cheque for $15,000. No arguments, no asking when I would repay it, nothing. Yes, there are people like that in the world. They are as rare as hen's teeth, but they are there. We did eventually start paying him back in regular instalments.

Starting that business from scratch, aligning the tradespeople, furniture, cosmetics, gowns, doing everything ourselves, was a phenomenal experience. It was the best thing that could have happened to me in regard to my future business coaching career. That sort of experience simply cannot be learned from books and I would not change it for the world.

- Chapter Twenty-Nine -
A Family Man

*"What is the appropriate behaviour for a man or
a woman in the midst of this world, where each person
is clinging to his piece of debris?
What's the proper salutation between people
as they pass each other in this flood?"*

Buddha

I didn't want children until after I was thirty. I didn't want to put any child through the experiences I'd had. When I eventually hit thirty, suddenly I really wanted children. I made a conscious decision to meet and marry the 'right' man.

I had always been afraid to get married, after watching both my parents divorce and then go on to struggle with other relationships. I worried that if I got married, it would also end in divorce. At this point in my life, I decided that the way to solve this problem was to simply marry the right man. Yes, I know, it was very naïve.

My ideal man would be very family-oriented, as we would surely have several children. And he wouldn't have too much money to cloud the picture.

I met Shaun in Whistler at the end of 1998. We both had broken legs, and he made a quip about my nice footwear. We liked each other instantly. He was a young man, quite attractive and had a job looking after trees or some such thing, as well as fighting fires and surveying. He was from a very stable family and he wanted children. He sounded like just what I was looking for. Within six weeks, we were engaged.

I suggested to Shaun that we didn't worry about the wedding just yet, and instead concentrate on having children. He was fully in agreement. Little did I know of the dark nights to follow. I had spent so many years trying not to get pregnant and then, when I wanted to get pregnant, it wasn't as easy as I thought it would be! Somebody was surely having a laugh upstairs.

I felt each and every conception. My first conception was the very first time we tried, on a camping trip. It was like tiny fluttering fireworks that began at my toes and went all the way up to the top of my head. I woke Shaun to tell him, 'It's happened, I am pregnant, or rather, "we" are pregnant.' Of course, most people hearing this in the middle of the night would simply laugh and go back to sleep. That is exactly what Shaun did. The next day, I went to the doctor and I told him I was pregnant. Of course he asked me how far along I was, and when I said one day, he laughed as well.

Once the pregnancy was confirmed, Shaun and I became really excited and began to plan for the birth. We hoped for a natural water-birth. I had attended one and found it just the most incredible experience. Shaun asked, 'What will I be doing? Will I be making you lots of tea?' It was so adorable. He didn't really know too much about birthing, but he wanted to learn. He even learned to cook, which was really handy, as up until then neither of us could cook at all.

That was when I was first starting the spa business and was the general contractor on-the-job. I was working eighteen-hour days on the remodelling and refurbishing, and was also studying for a homeopathic exam. I was very sick from the pregnancy, sometimes four or five times a day.

At nearly twenty weeks, I lost the child, probably because of the stress of all the work. We had named the baby Charlie, whether it was to be a boy or a girl. I miscarried at home, and we buried him beneath the tree that stood behind a sheer rock cliff overlooking the valley. It was a place we used to stop on our walks, just to pause a while and think about life.

I was completely devastated. Four of my friends were pregnant at the same time as me and so not long afterwards I was able to hold their newborn babies. Picking up one of the tiny beautiful bundles, I felt like someone had knifed me in the heart. I had to give them back to their mums as I cried inside for the loss of the child I never got to hold.

There were no baby sounds in my house, just the heaviness of the air itself. After the separation from my family, my brother taking his life, and my father's death, I truly believed that this soul had touched down and then not wanted to be with me. I could not get past it.

I so wanted to have my mum around at this difficult time, yet I had not spoken with her in a long while. I wished that I could tell her how I felt about what was happening in my life and connect with her again.

We decided to give baby-making a break and focus on something positive. Organising a wedding should take the focus off the pain I felt losing my baby.

- Chapter Thirty -
Husbands, Wives And Children

"Adopt the pace of nature: her secret is patience."
Ralph Waldo Emerson

Our original wedding ceremony was in Byron Bay on Nov 8th, 2002, when I was thirty five. It could not have been more perfect; it was better than I could have dreamed. We were married by a Buddhist monk right on the beach, with about twenty of our closest friends and family present.

Mum and I finally reconnected at the wedding, and began to develop a relationship. We began a process of talking, feeling, trying to understand each other, and more talking.

I wore a really simple dress that had a mermaid feel to it. It was grey satin with a diaphanous stole playing around my shoulders; just beautiful. There was a path laid with pebbles and flags, a large banner flaring in the wind, and a saxophonist playing the most beautiful music. It was one of the happiest days of my life, but I did not want to change my name.

We had another wedding ceremony in Canada, because we had so many Canadian friends and family that could not come to Australia for the wedding. For this ceremony we had First Nations rings made, full of ancient history. They represented two lives merging forever with eagles in flight, and were very tribal. There were about fifty people at this wedding, including about fifteen family. It was held on a gorgeous property in Owl Ridge on a beautiful summer's day. It was so much more relaxing than the first wedding, as we had done it all before.

We moved into a small cottage in town, and I worked

in the spa while Shaun became an occasional worker. I ran the house, paid the bills and hoped for a child.

After our wedding, we again tried to have children, but it was the same story. Two pregnancies back-to-back. Both times I lost the baby at about twenty weeks. My midwife became so anxious that I would not carry my babies, that she hesitated to call me whenever I told her I was pregnant. In the end, I had six pregnancies and one child.

My gynaecologist recommended Shaun and I be tested and I took the tests after the third miscarriage, but Shaun was still hesitant.

I found out that I had the blood condition Antiphospholipid Syndrome, and anti-nucleic antibodies. My gynaecologist recommended that we think about adopting a child, or perhaps using a donor bank. Apparently our bodies did not combine well. It was like mixing coffee and tea together, it just didn't work. Perhaps if we mixed up the balance by using a donor, we would get a different reaction.

Shaun and I could not afford adoption, and spent at least a year considering the impact on our relationship before deciding to use a donor bank. Once we had finally agreed, I travelled to Salt Lake City to have the insemination. When I got there, Shaun said he could no longer support me in this decision, so I agreed not to go ahead with it and came home again.

We didn't have another option, as we could not afford adoption, and after another year, Shaun was ready to try again. I decided to wait a few more months to make sure that this was really the decision he wanted. I got the go-ahead and went back to Salt Lake City to do the insemination. By this stage, I was at the end of my tether emotionally and didn't care if I had a child or not.

When I arrived at Salt Lake City, I was told that I should do three inseminations. I was so emotionally strained that after the first insemination, I had had enough. This only gave me a less than 5% chance of conceiving. I had to take my chances, and felt that if I were meant to have a child then it would work.

I felt that conception too, even though it was the weakest of all of my conceptions. Rather than a rush of fireworks, a pounding heart or a feeling of swimming in sperm, it felt like the gentlest of breaths on soft skin, barely noticeable. I thought to myself that there was no way this child would carry, it was simply too subtle.

However, it did happen. When I was three days pregnant I went to see the most amazing traditional Chinese medical practitioner, a man by the name of Sunny Lee. He was able to confirm my pregnancy and also let me know that it was a boy.

Sunny said that in order for me to carry, I needed to stay as calm as possible. That wasn't easy for someone like me, energetic and enthusiastic by nature.

Every time I got past a previous landmark when one of the other miscarriages had happened, fourteen weeks, sixteen weeks, and eighteen weeks, I was internally grateful and relieved. We prepared the baby's room with an air of hope and positivity.

Once again, I suffered terribly from morning sickness. Not just a little retching; this was projectile vomit. It would come instantly, even while I was talking or driving. If a car was driving too close, they would cop it on their windshield. I was sick until I got to twenty weeks. One snowy day, I had eaten raspberry pancakes. I had to stop right in the middle of the road to be sick. Puking out bright red berry pancakes on pristine white snow looked so bad, people were turning away as they drove past. It was pretty gross!

At sixteen weeks, I was rushed to St Paul's hospital because my blood levels had tripled. Several doctors agreed that it would not be possible for me to carry a healthy child. My child would have low birth weight, or be unhealthy, premature, have Downs Syndrome, or be deformed, because of my blood levels. After three hours of tests and questions, I was told I needed to take Warfarin three times a day. Warfarin is a powerful blood thinner, and is one of the main ingredients in rat poison.

It simply did not make sense to me. Even though the doctors were adamant, I did not feel right about it. I raced across the road, almost getting hit by a truck on my way to see Sunny Lee. When I arrived, I was in quite a state of panic, screaming, yelling and crying. Sunny told me to calm down, he would see me immediately.

When I told him what had happened, he said that if I took the medication my child would most likely be aborted. What to do? What to do? Whether I chose to take the medication or not, it seemed that something would happen to end my pregnancy.

I did not know how to move forward – how to make the 'right' choice and have faith that this was going to work and I would actually have a healthy pregnancy. It seemed that my long sought-after dream of holding a baby in my arms was once again slipping through my fingers. I was going to have to take my chances, but which way should I go?

I spent nine days in a state of panic, my heart racing all day, not sleeping, thoughts spinning constantly around in my head. Eventually I decided that I had to go with the person I trusted most, Sunny. That decision gave my child life.

Sunny's recommendation was for me to simply take a tablespoon of vinegar morning and night until a month after my pregnancy. Would you believe, it actually worked!

Ten days before my due date, I was rear-ended in a car accident. I sustained lower, middle and upper back injuries and nerve damage to my right arm. Injuries that would need many years of chiropractic, physiotherapeutic and acupuncture treatment. For the last ten days of my pregnancy, I cried every day, I was so anxious and upset. I had come so far; would I ever hold my baby?

I planned to have a home water-birth with a midwife. Lots of people thought I was nuts giving birth at home, but I knew it was the place I would feel most empowered. I wanted an experience that was positive, not fear-driven. I had interviewed eleven obstetricians and midwives before settling on my support team, which also included a Doula, Victoria, who was a close friend.

About a week before my due date, Shaun got some money from a settlement from his previous divorce and we decided to go out to dinner. It might be our last chance for a while. We had a lovely meal and Shaun got quite drunk so I drove home, where we settled down to watch Russell Crowe in the movie, *Master and Commander*.

As nature would have it, I felt my first contraction only a few minutes into the movie. I said to Shaun, 'The baby's coming', to which he replied, 'You can't be sure'. The contractions were so strong that I dug my fingernails into his arm. Even though he was quite drunk, he realised I might be right.

I called my midwife and Victoria, and Shaun suggested that I have a bath, which was a great idea. On the way to our house, the midwife had to stop at the scene of a car accident where a young man died. This must have been distressing for her, but I never knew that night, she was so calming and professional.

I had done a lot of pregnancy yoga, and this helped me to stay calm and fairly relaxed in the first stages of labour. As the pain increased though, I started to think I wouldn't be able to do it. It was like a strong period pain multiplied by a million. I tried to let the whole process go and just relax, but was still terrified that I would have a stillborn child. My midwife was so understanding, and checked the baby's heart rate whenever I asked. I couldn't believe the baby was so steady and relaxed all the way through.

I spent a long time in the bath, moving slowly like a giant aquatic creature. A water-birth was absolutely the right choice for me, I was so glad I decided to press ahead with this decision despite other people's concerns.

Once my water broke, I got out of the bath and anchored myself over the couch, where the baby was born an hour later. There was no pause between the head birthing and then the body, he came all at once, like a little freight train. It was 7 am on June 25th, 2004. Once he was born, he screamed the house down and I thought to myself, 'Oh, there is a baby in the house!' I didn't register for a moment that it was my baby!

When the baby lay on my chest, I was so worried that I would suffocate him. The midwife said to me, 'The baby is OK, but Mummy needs to breathe'. We had chosen the name Sebastian for a boy, but once he was born we changed our minds. It didn't help that the young man who had been killed in the accident the midwife had stopped at, had been called Sebastian. The midwife said afterwards that she felt that because the Angel of Death had visited, this meant that our baby would be OK.

So for the first five weeks the baby's name was Dylan, but that didn't suit him either. Then we settled on Jacob, which he kept until he was four months old. Finally, we found the right name for our special child, Jaiesh. It is pronounced *Jay Esh*, and means 'light' in Sanskrit and 'courage' in Arabic.

Jaiesh had his first homeopathic remedy at thirteen days old, Chamomile and then Pulsatilla. Mind you, the skin outbreak he had from the second dose made his head look like it was covered in stale cornflakes. He looked like something out of Star Trek. I decided I had better get some professional advice in treating babies!

I took Jaiesh with me to work each day, and Shaun worked occasionally, as well as spending a lot of time watching sport on the telly, eating pizza and in general being in an obliging mood if left alone. But he called me every day, asking how I was, and more specifically, where I was. I was touched.

He wasn't much help with the baby, and I felt like a single mum from the beginning. One thing I asked for over and over again was for Shaun to bath Jaiesh in the evenings. I think in that first year, it happened twice.

I had no idea of the demons my husband was battling, but when our son was a year old it all came to a head. It finally all made sense – the trouble with our fertility, the trouble with our marriage, the lack of interaction between father and son, the reluctance to come to appointments with the midwife.

- Chapter Thirty-One -
Discovery Of A Different Identity

"Always keep an open mind and a compassionate heart."
Phil Jackson

I was nearly thirty nine when Jaiesh had his first birthday. I made a tofu cheesecake as his birthday cake, an unusual choice perhaps, but I am a health food junkie by nature.

I had accidentally left it sitting on the stove at home, so I had to come back to pick it up. My husband and I shared a truck, but rather than phone him to pick me up, I just borrowed my business partner's car to pop home.

As I opened the front door of our house, I saw a flash of pink. I could hear Shaun speaking on the phone, finishing a job interview. But it didn't sound like his regular voice. As I turned the corner from the hall into the kitchen and living area, I saw him standing there, wearing one of my favourite sets of lacy underwear. It was a beautiful black demi-cup bra and lacy g-string, and was set off by a pair of my pink high-heeled shoes.

I froze. My mind went in a million different directions. Was I in someone else's house? Was this my husband? Was it a joke? Was it a kinky sex thing I wasn't getting? My brain could not compute what was happening.

He looked ridiculous, there was nothing to fill the top and too much hanging out the bottom. Should I laugh? Was it a fetish? Did my husband like to dress up? I had thought he was so conservative and traditional. In that moment, my cheesecake world was turned upside down. I suddenly realised that everything before must have been a lie. It was as though my head had been cut in half, part of my brain removed and put back in, upside down.

I must have been holding my breath. He came over and

took my hand, shaking slightly. 'I thought for a moment about lying to you, but the truth is, I have always wanted to be a girl.'

I immediately and instinctively put the wife and mother gently aside and went into homoeopathic counselling mode. It was the only way I could get through this. I was shocked to my core and couldn't take it all in. But I thought that if I said the wrong thing, I could destroy the person standing in front of me. I needed to be fully present and fully compassionate. I looked him up and down and said, 'You are going to be a beautiful girl. Help yourself to my clothes.' Then I picked up the cheesecake and ran out the door.

I will never get that image out of my mind. The effort he had gone to, to keep his secret from me and the world, must have been massive. I am not a person that notices small details, and realised that he must have been putting my lingerie back in my drawer without me noticing it had been handled. Whenever I went out, he would ask me when I'd be home. That obviously was the time he dressed up. I'd just thought he was being caring and organised. His dad was a banker, his mum a nurse, and they had seemed such a sensible, stable family.

If I hadn't come home unexpectedly that day, would I have ever known? Nobody had guessed the truth, not even my mum, who usually has a sixth sense about things. There was no use berating myself. I simply did not know.

Three days after this tragic discovery, Shaun, devastated by guilt and shame, drove himself to the base of Wedge Mountain and tried to gas himself in the car. He said that the only reason he had lived, was that my dead brother, Daniel, had visited him and said, 'You can't do this to my sister. You can't.' Although Shaun was quite sick from inhaling the fumes, he did live, thank goodness.

Being transgender is a challenge in most societies, and caused incredible complexities in our family dynamics. It is so important for people to follow their own path, and to accept themselves and others, for their differences and for being just as they are. I didn't hold any ill will towards Shaun, and spent a lot of time healing myself and the wound this had all caused. He would need a lot of love and courage on this path. Unfortunately, his parents disowned him as soon as they found out. He did continue to have the support and love of his aunt, uncle and cousins, which was wonderful.

For a while, Shaun went to work as a fire-fighter and surveyor during the day, and then came home and dressed up as Rene at night. Jaiesh was in bed by the time Rene would come out. Although I was very compassionate to the situation on hand, I wasn't coping emotionally.

I had a one-year-old son, 35 staff in a failing business with a toxic business partnership, and a husband who wanted to be a woman. My mind could not hold all these priorities, never mind process them, and after four months I asked Shaun to leave. He moved to Vancouver to discover himself, while I was left penniless in Whistler, unable even to pay the rent.

Over the next eighteen months, we met regularly for Adlerian transgender counselling, which really helped us both. First we worked through the issues around Shaun being transgender, and then I started having counselling for 'complicated grief' which is what happens when your husband comes out as transgender and then makes the transition into their 'genuine self'. In this case, Shaun became Rene. It was as if my husband had died, because I never got to see or be with him again, and was instead trying to get to know a new woman. I was awash with so many emotions: sadness, anger, grief and betrayal.

My core belief was that if I loved and grew attached to something, then bad things would happen. This had been demonstrated to me with losing my mother at such a young age, my horse being sold, and then Daniel's death. Through Adlerian therapy I was able to reprogram myself to truly believe, deep inside, that if I was happy, good things would happen to me.

A lot of water went under the bridge and Rene and I eventually became friends. We even began to giggle about things. One day, when I was invited out on a date, Rene offered to do my hair and make-up. The awful thing was that she was really good at it.

She became much happier once her outside matched her inside. She had always known the truth, yet never allowed herself to be her authentic self. I am so proud of her and only wish her the best. The Adlerian therapy and an amazing therapist gave me back the keys to my life and I have been on an upward spiral ever since.

While we were in counselling, I started to see the character of my husband disintegrate, while this new woman emerged. To say it was a fascinating process does not do it justice; it was tragic and amazing all at the same time. Ultimately, I am attracted to men, not women, and so our relationship ended, while we remained good friends. Rene's personality was different to the man I married, and two years later there was nothing left of my husband.

- Chapter Thirty-Two -
House-Sitting

"Where there is love there is life."
Mahatma Gandhi

My sister generously lent me $5,000, which paid my rent for a couple of months. I couldn't continue to borrow money for rent, and started to consider house-sitting, just temporarily until the business started to make money again. I had no inkling it would turn into three years.

I was in denial about the business failing, stressed about my marriage and Shaun's issues, looking after a one-year-old child, and trying to pay my staff. As things started to spiral out of control, I began to make poor decisions. Once the spiral began, the poor decisions and the denial became worse until I was so removed from myself I could not feel a thing. I became anaesthetised to the disaster my life had become.

I started to wear the same pair of army camouflage pants every single day. They were my suit of armour, my protection against the outside world. They were not being washed often, and as time went on, the need to wash them just fell away, it was simply another thing I chose not to deal with.

My life had come down to the basics of food and shelter.

Jaiesh and I lived on dahl and rice for most of those three years. Mung beans or lentils were only $5 a bag, and rice was only $2. This was enough to last about three weeks. They are considered Ayurvedic whole foods, and were so healthy and affordable that I can't understand why people use the excuse that they live on takeaway because they can't afford healthy food.

I took on an early morning cleaning job at a local

restaurant, so I could cover the staff wages at the spa. I woke Jaiesh at four in the morning and took him to the restaurant. We would turn the music up really loud as I got stuck into sweeping, vacuuming and mopping the floors. Jaiesh was delighted as he was able to drink fruit juice, something I could not afford.

I found house-sitting to be a very stressful way to live. I never knew how many nights we could stay, and would rush to clean and tidy the house before the owners returned, packing gear into the truck and moving on to the next place. There was still staff training and payroll to do at the spa, clients to see, and the restaurant to clean in the mornings. Sometimes I would curl up to sleep on the futon in the shiatsu room at the spa with my little son beside me, then have a shower in the morning and get back into it all again.

Sometimes I would cry myself to sleep and wish to never again wake up. I honestly don't know how I kept going, I think it was just the determination to provide for my precious child. It would be years before I would be able to unwind from this, relax and actually feel again; emotions like happiness, contentment and even loneliness. I had created such a wall around myself in order to survive, that it took quite some time to break it down again. It has made me quite fearless though, and the warrior woman inside me now takes every opportunity by the horns.

Jaiesh was an angel. He never complained about eating the same thing every day, or moving from house to house. These days, of course, he has much more choice, but choice does not necessarily make him a happier boy. When our lives were so basic and simple, he did not ask for things; he was calmer in a way. There wasn't the absolute necessity to fill his time and space with material things. It was an interesting journey. Now he is able to want for more, and to a certain extent his desire for stuff is insatiable. This is his lesson and he is learning.

I also learned a lot about making do with less. Nothing was ever purchased new, it was all clothes swaps, garage sales and charity shops. These lessons have stayed with me, and I am still very careful with money. I don't believe in mindlessly spending money simply because you have it.

Eventually, I got so exhausted from all the moving, that I borrowed my friend Victoria's two-man tent to live in. I was just glad to have a home for my boy and me.

- Chapter Thirty-Three -
Living In A Tent

"The truth is that our finest moments are most likely to occur when we are feeling deeply uncomfortable, unhappy, or unfulfilled. For it is only in such moments, propelled by our discomfort, that we are likely to step out of our ruts and start searching for different ways or truer answers."

M. Scott Peck

For three months in 2008, I pitched my little tent wherever I found a spot that was perfect and safe. No rent, no power bills. But also no warmth and nothing else – just a longing to be able to provide more for my child. I was so empty, my soul could run around inside and I would not feel anything but darkness, coldness and anxiety.

I was sitting in front of our makeshift home, the blue two-man tent, one cold autumn morning, cradling a cup of hot tea and feeling the dew as it kissed my bare toes. Feeling the earth with my bare feet helped give me some much needed stability. My camp stove was flickering blue and my son was sleeping. At times like these, I often thought that it might be a good idea to be a drinker. Mum had said it was her saviour. A glass here and there, the mellow softening of the mind, the quiet, the calm and most important, the forgetting. Perhaps it's best I never got into it!

I looked back over my life, and asked myself how this could possibly have happened to me. I came from an affluent family, but I never felt it as a child. My friends at school thought we were rich because my dad was a doctor. I never remember getting a new fridge, washer or dryer. While Dad did upgrade his cars regularly, he kept to the tried and trusted Japanese models which were nothing fancy. Yet, I do remember that we always had whatever we wanted.

I went to good schools, had some great corporate jobs and got a few letters after my name. So how on earth had I wound up homeless, living in a tent, cleaning floors and living hand-to-mouth?

What was the catalyst? Was it my brother's suicide? The rejection and all the other traumas throughout my childhood? Or a combination of these? Or none of them? I didn't have an answer.

I knew I would have to change things soon. I watched my friends take their kids to swimming lessons, buy them clothes, take them on outings, and offer them different things to eat. I was offering none of that to my beautiful boy.

I would watch him sleeping in the tent, the sound of his breathing calming my soul, as tears streamed down my cheeks. My life felt like it was over, and yet I had this amazing living, breathing and loving boy who had chosen me as his mum. I had to somehow give him a life worth living.

My business partner knew about my transient living arrangements and the state of my marriage. When I told her that I was now living in a tent, she just laughed. Our business partnership was already on the rocks, but our other divide was that she never felt the pain of the failing business because her lifestyle remained the same. She had a husband who supported her, new clothes, new jewellery, a warm and comfortable house, with two happy children.

Sitting in front of my borrowed tent on that cold morning, I knew I had to make a move, but the lethargy of emotional exhaustion was paralysing. It seemed enough just to sit there, looking into the blue flickering flame and letting my tea go cold. But I had to move. My son needed a warm home with a proper bed, the camping adventure was over. I needed to finish the disastrous partnership in the spa, find a reasonable place to live, make some serious money and in short, start all over again.

I so wanted a normal relationship, with a normal man, who had no hidden secrets, and liked me just as I was. Working together towards a common goal, just being normal together. Was I aiming too high? And anyway, what is 'normal'? I remember my dad saying there was no normal, it was just a perception, like beauty.

All my friends but one were avoiding me like the plague. It seemed that poverty was catching. We instinctively avoid the homeless and cross the road rather than confront it. It just goes to show how hardship is handled in general by our society, how we cope with the curve balls life throws at us. If you must fall by the wayside, you will be doing it alone.

I spent years in analysis, immersing myself in self knowledge, to advance myself spiritually and gain insight into getting the most out of life. But it seemed that all the books I read focussed on achieving the peaks, getting to the top of the mountain ahead of everyone else. No one talked about just 'being'. What about the simple satisfaction of being born, going to school, having a job, getting married, having kids and growing old? Being happy and content just living an ordinary life? Perhaps achieving these seemingly small goals is not as ordinary as I had first thought. Perhaps what I had thought was ordinary, was actually extraordinary?

- Chapter Thirty-Four -
The Turning Point

"There is a powerful driving force inside every human being that once unleashed can make any vision, dream, or desire a reality."

Anthony Robbins

At the beginning of September, Mum rang me. She was really sick, and getting sicker. She'd been prescribed a cocktail of pills and couldn't take three steps without having to catch her breath. She was over medicated and it was slowly killing her. I knew I had to go home.

I had looked for something to move me forward, and here it was. Once I knew where I was going, once I had a goal, it started to take shape. A lady I was studying homeopathy with, offered me enough frequent flyer points for my ticket to Australia. I started telephoning around to find some money to get another ticket for my son.

I called my old bookkeepers, hoping they'd help me as they had helped me before. They were incredible, loaning me $10,000 with no due date for repayment. They were a retired couple who lived in a mobile home. The kindness that humans are capable of astounds me at times.

Four days after Mum's call, my son and I were on a flight to Australia. It took about five months of constant care, research and trial and error before Mum's health began to return.

I was on a journey to help my mum as well as heal my relationship with her. I also wanted to build something between her and Jaiesh, so he could have the benefit of having a grandparent.

Mum shared her one-bedroom apartment with Jaiesh and me. When I was house-sitting, people had suggested that I move back with my mother, but I had thought it was a ridiculous idea. I was an adult, and a mother! Now, coming home to that small unit every day was such a comfort. Having somewhere regular to stay, where I belonged, was an amazing feeling after not belonging anywhere for so long.

We took turns sleeping on the bed, the couch and the floor. Sometimes, on hot nights, I would take the cushions off the couch and lay them on the floor with a blanket over them, so I could spread out a bit. My wardrobe was the back of the bedroom door – I had so few clothes I could just hang them there. Luckily Mum and I were a similar size and could share some outfits.

We didn't have any money of course, and luxuries were few and far between. We definitely weren't in an abundance mindset! Mum knew how I loved soft cheeses like Brie and Camembert, but of course it was out of our budget.

One day, as a treat, she bought a King Island Double Cream Brie for me. At $6 this was a pretty wild purchase. She could barely wait until I got home to offer it to me. 'Here you are, crumpet, one of your favourites', she said proudly. I looked at her and then at that beautiful, soft, runny Brie and without a flicker of thought said, 'I don't feel like it'. Something shifted inside Mum, I could see the hot rush of anger creeping up in her. She snatched the cheese from the kitchen counter, took a good swing and chucked it into the garbage. Then she turned and walked away. I suddenly realised what I had done and ran after her, the rescued cheese in one hand and a big smile on my face. 'See Mum, here it is. I really like it. Look, I am eating it now.' I quickly peeled back the foil and took a bite. She couldn't help but laugh.

The housing commission block we lived in was filled with ladies of all backgrounds and mental descriptions. The ladies in the front few units didn't like the way the ladies in the back units did the garden, so they got up in the middle of the night to pull out all the plants. The lady downstairs couldn't speak at all, but seemed to have super human strength and pulled out her entire kitchen, counter tops and all, with her bare hands. Her ancient boyfriend would drink all day, slouched by the front door, waiting for her to come home. They seemed to find some solace in each other in their little apartment with no kitchen, and only a couple of mattresses on the floor for furniture.

Then there was the Spanish lady next door who spoke in very broken English, although she had been here for 40 years. Her daughter lived in the front units and they were always fighting. I could hear their arguments in Spanish as it scraped across bricks and windowsills. Hot and sweaty, I closed the windows for some peace.

Mum was anxious all the time, worried that the landlords would discover there was more than one person living in our apartment. When things got heated between us, I would go and stay with friends for a few days. Our relationship was always backwards and forwards, backwards and forwards, and yet she loved me so deeply, as only a mother could. She shared her small space with us, and secretly pawned her jewellery so we had enough money for food. When I was having trouble falling pregnant, she even offered to carry a baby for me. Unconditional love, what a lesson.

Eventually I got on my feet and was able to get my own two-bedroom place in Centennial Park. In our apartment we didn't have a bath, so I bought a big red plastic bucket to bathe Jaiesh in. It was so cute to see him curled up in there. I was not disappointed when we upgraded the bucket to a full sized tub in my new space. I bought him his very first bed, but even now he chooses to sleep on the floor a lot of the time, or snuggled up in bed with me.

As Mum's health continued to improve, I really wanted to find a job, but did not want to be separated from my son. I wanted to make sure that I had enough time for him, but still have an income.

Up until now, I hadn't been asking myself the right questions to change my life. While it was all about me and my problems, I kept thinking it would somehow get better, and in the meantime I could just keep on going. I wasn't forced to make changes. But when I started looking after Mum it stopped being about me, and started being about my mum, so I just got on with caring for her and did what had to be done. It really opened my eyes to the fact that I wasn't making any positive change in my own life.

I talked to Mum about how I could change the rut I was in, but I couldn't consider giving up the spa. The staff there were like my children, I felt responsible to continue paying their wages rather than letting them go. Perhaps sometimes the universe knows when you need to make a change, even when you can't make it yourself.

My business partner was calling me every day, badgering me about being in Australia while she was left in charge. By February, she had had enough of running everything on her own, and asked me to give the business over to her. It was such a hard decision to make after giving ten years of my life and putting so much of myself into it. If I gave the business to her, I would never get anything back on my investment. I had probably lost the better part of a million dollars over the ten years. I spent three weeks thinking about it and realised that, if I was in her shoes, I'd want it too.

I signed the business over to her legally, and of course she paid me nothing for it. Then about a year later, she came to me asking for money to help keep the business running. I talked to my lawyer about it and he said, 'Look, you gave it to her. If you gave a car to someone, and a year later, they came asking for money to fix it, it would be the same. It's not your problem.' So I finally let it all go.

I can make up lots of excuses as to why our business didn't work. In the end, our business failed because I could not make the right decisions, and I did not take responsibility for changing our business partnership or getting a business partnership agreement.

I did learn to become a very creative thinker though, which got me out of a huge number of problems. I could find money when it was needed, pulling it out of thin air.

I also learned that a business should be built up either to sell, or for passive income. Building up a business just so you can keep working in it is just buying yourself a job. I learned that to be profitable, you should work 'on' a business, not 'in' it.

I had to move on to something else. I sat down to think about what I really wanted. As ridiculous as it sounded, I wanted to make $40,000 a month. I wrote this goal down on a piece of paper one night while I was crying in the tent. I have carried the piece of paper with me ever since. The end result may have seemed unachievable, but I took it one step at a time, slowly building confidence, slowly building a plan, believing I could make it. Eighteen months later, I had reached my goal.

- Chapter Thirty-Five -
Training To Be A Business Coach

"One of the things that may get in the way of people being lifelong learners is that they're not in touch with their passion. If you're passionate about what it is you do, then you're going to be looking for everything you can to get better at it."

Jack Canfield

While I was at the spa in Canada, a client had come in for a homeopathic consultation, and as we chatted she told me she was a business coach. I liked the idea of being a business coach as soon as I heard about it, and tucked it away in the back of my mind as a 'one day' thing. I still had the spa and thirty five employees, so I smiled to myself and thought it would never happen. It is really interesting what happens when you put a thought out there. Often it starts to work on its own to bring that reality to you.

Three years later, I was in Australia, looking for opportunities to start again. I called the woman I had met in Canada and told her that I was really interested in coaching. But at the same time, I was very fearful of doing it. Losing so much money over ten years in the spa had knocked my confidence and self-esteem.

I really needed a steady income to put food on the table and a roof over our heads, and couldn't afford to make another mistake. Starting out as a business coach would be a risk, with no guaranteed income, so I tried not to think about it and concentrate on my other options. I considered one job paying $70,000 a year and another where I had to travel to India once or twice a year. Both of these sounded attractive, but somehow I kept coming back to coaching. Of course despite not wanting to go towards it, coaching was in my mind all the time, and I ended up manifesting it anyway. Thinking about something all the time always brings it to you, even if what you are thinking is that you don't want it!

So I met up with Jody, the coach I met in Canada, and we talked it through. The coaching was with ActionCOACH, the leading business coaching company in the world. I knew that if I was going to go down this road, it had to be with the best company, so ActionCOACH was the only option. I couldn't afford another failure. Then I found out how much it would cost: $25,000 for the initial course in Las Vegas, plus of course the airfares and spending money – I did have to eat after all. It would cost around $30,000 in all. I nearly fell over. I had been making around $5000 a year for such a long time, it was ridiculous for me to even contemplate it. When I told Mum about it, even she thought it was too big an order. She said it would be too hard for me, too much stress after what I had been through; perhaps I should just get a regular job and not worry about it.

Then Jody offered to advance me half the money, if I could raise the other half. I think that if she had not offered to help, I would not have even tried. It was a pretty big call, but once I had decided to do it I tried everything possible. I knew in my heart I was meant to do this coaching. But how was I to come up with the money? I had nothing. Absolutely nothing.

Your own determination and dedication to change your situation will bring you something. However, it has to be you who reaches out, you have to make it happen.

I went to all the banks for a loan, but they weren't interested in someone with no job and no home. My financial record wasn't great, and I had only been in the country for three months. As I visited each bank, I started to get smart. I learned what it was they wanted me to write on the form in order to get a loan. For a loan of $25,000, I needed to have been in the country for a minimum of six months, and earn $80,000 per year. On my next application, magically I had been in the country for six months and earned $80,000. Creative thinking got me a loan for $15,000. With further persistence, I ended up with a swag of credit cards again. This time, it had to be worth it.

A friend lent me $1600 spending money, I borrowed some of Mum's clothes and I was off to Las Vegas.

The training was really rigorous and had been designed to show our habits and how we behave. This set us up well for coaching, to demonstrate how you must change your behaviour in order to get results. We started at 5 am with volleyball, and they changed the rules constantly as we went along. They were crazy rules, like only being able to hit the ball with your nose. Grown men were throwing tantrums, shouting and throwing water bottles around because the rules kept changing. After living in 40 houses in three years, I was so at home with change that I found it quite easy.

I was like a pig in mud; so happy, because I was having the opportunity to learn and grow rather than trying to put food on the table or find a place to live. I took in every word as I envisaged a new life for my mum, my son and myself. I missed my son terribly and the guilt of leaving him in Australia was almost unbearable, yet I knew that this was my big chance to create an amazing life.

At the end of the course we had a little ceremony where we shared our stories. I had a little cry when I talked about my life, after all, it had only been five months earlier that I was living in a tent off charity food handouts with my then four-year-old son. How far we can come, what we can achieve, if only we have the right mind-set – being positive, and willing to learn and grow. As they went around the room asking each participant who had inspired them the most, every single person said the same thing: that I was their biggest inspiration. I did not realise that I had made a difference to these people. So when I came back to Australia, for the first time in ten years I was starting to get a little confidence back. I finally had the possibility of a different future.

- Chapter Thirty-Six -
Starting A Coaching Business

"All the breaks you need in life wait within your imagination. Imagination is the workshop of your mind, capable of turning mind energy into accomplishment and wealth."
Napoleon Hill

When the training was over, I still had a lot to learn and so much more growing to do. I still had a very deep poverty mentality and was not able to fully grasp the idea of responsibility. I just could not understand the idea of wealth or abundance, those words were so foreign to me. I began to go into even more debt, and I was oblivious to the fact that I lived in a victim mentality.

I was lucky to train initially under another coach as I lacked both the funds and the confidence to do it myself, and wanted someone to guide me. I continued my pattern of drawing strong women to me until I finally learned to be strong for myself. The coaching agreement meant that in return for coaching clients, I received three hours free coaching for myself per week, as well as 40 to 50% of my earnings.

Although it was a great way to get started, soon I found it incredibly stifling and was back to that old feeling of being in a cage. How many times had I felt this in my lifetime? It had become all too comfortable, like an old pair of slippers, so easy to slip back into when things got hard. My confidence was so low I got very few clients, and my commission was so low, I made very little money. In the end though, the struggle I went through during this period helped me to become a better coach.

Originally I had signed a two-year contract to work under

the other coach, but after a year I couldn't stand it any more. Luckily, the woman I was working for could also see that it wasn't ideal, so we agreed to part. Not long afterwards, ActionCOACH asked me to come and work directly for them with my own licence, and I have never looked back. It was a huge gift, and gave me the freedom I needed to fly.

Once I went to work direct for ActionCOACH, I watched all the top performers in the company, and was trying to learn their coaching style, their behaviour, and how they found clients. In modelling myself on these top performers, I was trying to be something I was not. In the process, I was losing my unique abilities and my authenticity. The 'me' that I was becoming was not real or authentic, so everything was a struggle. I became very nervous and wound up, and simply could not relax, despite regular kinesiology sessions.

I was trying to learn new skills and immersing myself in a new system. The learning and growing that I had to do became overwhelming. There were days that I secretly wished to be back in my tent, anaesthetised to hard work and learning. I was lonely and wanted friendship and company. Letting go of the beliefs and behaviours that no longer served me took all my energy and left me feeling empty. I was becoming a blank canvas, but had no idea what masterpiece to paint in the space I had created. My boy needed the opportunity for a new life, I was desperate for change and committed to figuring out how to become the best coach I could.

Three months into the coaching, I still did not have a client. I was starting to panic. I was still living with my mum, had spent all that money on the training and still had no clients and no money coming in.

One of the reasons I was struggling with coaching was because I did not have enough self worth or self-confidence to ask a client to make a financial commitment to their coaching, even for a month. I would get so shaky asking them if they would like to pay for their coaching, that it would repulse them and they were soon out the door. The truth is that I would not have put my faith in me as a coach back then, so how could I expect a paying client to put their faith in me?

I was excited and nervous to have set up a meeting with a potential client, when a good friend asked me out to lunch. I protested because I wanted to focus on the meeting, but he convinced me not just to go to the lunch, but even to have a couple of glasses of wine. I don't usually drink when I am working, but when I came back to the office that day, I was in a very happy mood.

The wine had given me a calmness where usually I would be so anxious. Suddenly, I found myself chatting with the client about her private life, her business, where the business could and should go. She asked me when she could start and how much it would cost for a year's coaching. I was almost speechless, I was completely unprepared for this and just about fell off my chair. A year of coaching paid upfront? Are you kidding? I wondered if she too had a few drinks with her lunch as I tried to work out the cost. I gave her a big discount, which went against my training, but I found it so hard to deal with a lump sum that large. I had a client!

This was the turning point for me. I realised that being relaxed had been the key, so I worked at just being myself and not trying so hard. It was a huge revelation. From that point onwards, I decided not to take monthly clients, only six- or twelve-month blocks. When people are financially committed to that extent, it tends to produce extraordinary results.

From then on, I found it easy to find new clients. I started to get bigger clients who in turn got bigger results. I attracted lots of media publicity, and before I knew it I was ranked number four coach worldwide. I am working on being number one. I want to push myself to the limits and be the best I can be. I want to know what the fibre of my being is.

Coaching has helped me to take responsibility for myself and my actions. If you don't take responsibility for your life, you are in denial, a victim. If you take responsibility for your life, you are a victor making positive moves. Through coaching, I have the opportunity to show others how empowering it is to realise that your entire life is a product of the decisions you make, and the changes you make.

Coaching has opened so many possibilities for me. It has helped me change so many lives for the better. I wake up every morning and I ask myself how I can leverage myself, how I can do more with less. Thinking in that paradigm has been so powerful for me. If you want to move a huge boulder, you know you cannot move it with your hands. But if you had a lever, it would be no problem. That's how I look at my business, at my life. Creating ever greater, more amazing possibilities with little or no effort, through finding the right catalyst.

That is what I teach through my coaching and through my retreats – to have the mind-set to create dreams and make them real. When I started the retreats 15 years ago, I had only planned to do one course. It filled within 30 minutes, and now I do a couple a year, and have just opened them up in Australia. The retreats developed a life of their own and are constantly being improved by my team and myself.

Life is a series of unexpected changes. Sunny and easy today, grey tomorrow. The more we can adapt to it all, the better life will be. One of the quotes that got me through tough times is, 'The darkest hour is before dawn and the dawn is always so beautiful'. The greatest learning is done in this darkness, so it is important to not rush it. It is important to take your time and get the valuable lessons. When you break through, you will have had time to recognise your purpose, your self and your soul. Then you can open up to your true journey. I am so lucky to travel with my clients as they discover this world of possibility.

I really enjoy observing my clients, watching their behaviours, asking why they are doing well or not so well, how they walk in the door, how they sit down, how they speak to me, how they present themselves. I really am a human behaviour detective. This observation process has been a great tool in helping people in their businesses.

One client I saw had issues with money – she just loved to spend it! It was really affecting her life in many ways, and causing great conflict with her husband. When she was able to recognise how she was sabotaging her life, she began to contemplate spending less. When she felt the urge to spend, instead of buying a new BMW, she would just buy a handbag. Soon her husband stopped worrying about her behaviour, and when she went on an overseas trip he gave her the green light to buy whatever she wanted. She came back with one bottle of perfume. She had been so triggered by being told she couldn't do something, that she had rebelled. Once the thrill of being mischievous was gone, the game was over.

Assisting clients to set goals, build a plan and measure achievements is all very well, but if you don't understand how people are motivated or which areas they struggle with, then you can't make the deep cognitive shifts at the core of their thought processes that are needed for real change.

A friend once said to me that she would never be coached by me because I had such a huge failure with my own business. I responded that I would never be coached by someone who had not failed and then gone on to succeed, because the greatest lessons are in that failure. I want to be coached by someone who has seen the good times and the bad.

I see obstacles coming up in people's businesses that could cause them real problems, and I slow them down so they can deal with these things before they explode. I like to lay thick, solid paths to keep the business strong and on track. I can also see possibilities that aren't always obvious.

I worked with a builder who was nearly bankrupt when he came to me. He needed a project manager but couldn't afford one with the 15 years experience he thought was essential to do the job properly. Instead, I helped him to see a greater possibility for his company's future by bringing in a less experienced project manager at a lower salary. We had a phenomenal outcome, and within twelve months of coaching, his business was turning over in excess of $2.2 million.

Another client's business was suffering because of a lack of structure in his industry. He could not see that structure was needed, because he had never experienced it before. Once we had discussed the need for structure, things started to change, and soon he met a person who just happened to be developing a template for his industry.

We can be limited by the possibilities that we see in front of us. We may be swimming in a teacup or the Indian Ocean, depending on our perception. Limited thinking just means you go round and round in the teacup.

- Chapter Thirty-Seven -
Ego vs Soul

"The greater part of most people's thinking is involuntary, automatic and repetitive. It is no more than a kind of mental static and fulfils no real purpose. Strictly speaking, you don't think, thinking happens to you. The statement 'I think' implies volition. It implies that you have a say in the matter, that there is choice involved on your part. For most people, this is not yet the case. 'I think' is just as false a statement as 'I digest' or 'I circulate blood'. Digestion happens, circulation happens, thinking happens."

Eckhart Tolle

I just love this quote. All of a sudden you are asking yourself: 'Well, if thinking just happens to me, then what am I doing and what am I controlling?' Many people would assume that their importance or significance has been taken away.

In all reality, being 'you' has more to do with your essence, your true nature, than your identity. Imagine living in a space where you don't need to try, you can just 'be'. A space where you don't worry about judgements from yourself, or others. A space which is smooth and seamless, that knows no bounds. When you are coming from ego there is a certain part of you that has desire, or a need to 'fill up'. Why do you think we have so many issues in our society with addiction, crime etc? These are all from a place of ego. A place where the ego does not have enough, a place where the ego's desires are all-consuming.

The problem here is that, when ego takes over, you will never be 'full'. The filling up is never-ending, so you simply seek greater means to do it. Spending more money, sleeping with more people, taking more drugs, getting thinner, stronger or having greater wealth. This to me is what I call a 'young' soul. This is a soul that is still enamoured with the physical, having not yet realised that none of these things will last and none of them can be taken with you into the next life.

What your soul (the essence of you, that which animates you) needs, is to realise its full potential on this planet and to live from a place of being completely full. Full of love, light and abundance. It also needs to live from a place that is harmonic, i.e. a place that is completely in unison with the rest of the planet and all living entities.

We need to relax, let go, stop trying and start to observe. Observe how we feel, what we are doing, when we feel content. What effect we are having when we come from this place. Remember you are here to have this experience called life.

How do we know the difference between what is ego and what is soul?

Let's look at some definitions, this may make it easier. Ego is the 'self', that which we see in our mind. It is pride, conceit or the image of self. The conscious mind if you like. Soul, on the other hand, is a deeply felt emotion, that which animates us, our spiritual nature, or that part of us which is immortal. Can you see the difference?

One has a use-by-date and is only concerned with the superficial here and now. The other is more about your true nature, the way you express yourself and show up in the world. Think of the movie *Avatar*, and you will start to have an inkling about the concept I am trying to explain. Every living entity in the world is connected to and from each other, energetically, sometimes physically and sometimes cyclically like the seasons. There is a rhythm or a pattern to everything. Every living entity also impacts the natural life and daily functioning of all other life forms. We are all interdependent.

Each and every day, we impact our world, our animals, our atmosphere and our environment. Most of the time, we are not conscious of this. The way we impact these biospheres is usually negative.

How do we start to impact the world in a more positive way?

We need to start to understand ourselves, to ever have any hope of understanding another or understanding the way we impact our world.

In short, we need to be more aware and more conscious of everything we do, every intent we have, right down to the smallest thought that crosses our mind. All these thoughts carry energy and we want to emanate our essence, our being, from the most positive place that we can.

The simplest way to do this is to have love for all. When you come from a place of love, your energy shifts dramatically. Rather than being defensive, you live more from a space of kindness, understanding and abundance for all living beings. If we all went about our daily lives with the intention of loving every person or animal we connected with, the energy shift on the planet would be palpable. We would feel it. All it takes is a tiny shift in intent, a tiny shift towards our soul, a tiny shift away from 'me' and towards 'I'.

When we all begin to understand that power in our own life, which is all about releasing the 'me ego' and harnessing our very own 'I' (soul) in a unique truth, then the possibility for a planet of peace and harmony becomes real. This, of course, is a process and it is a constant process of staying in pro action and not succumbing to reaction. Pro action is soul, reaction is ego.

You can *feel* the ego when you react. This might be when you react to someone who cuts you off in the traffic, or someone who says something nasty about you, or someone who hits you. Anger is from ego, and anger rises up because of your own false impression of the importance and significance that you have in your own life.

Would you be mad if the traffic had slowed to a halt, the

temperature was 40°C and your air conditioning had stopped, then someone had just pushed into the lane in front of you, almost wiping out the front of your car? Would you really be mad? Yes? If you say yes, then this is your ego reacting, this is your sense of your own self-importance reacting.

Now, I know this may seem a little hard to understand, so let me explain a bit further. Imagine you then found out that in the back seat of the car that had so rudely swung in front of you, almost taking out your headlights, there was a small boy who was bleeding to death and if he did not make it to the hospital in the next two minutes he would surely die. I am sure, now that you know what is REALLY going on, you would not have any reaction to the situation. You would pray for the child to reach the hospital. Pray that he is saved and you may even think of a way to get him there faster.

Part of the reason that your ego would now be okay with this is because the situation that just arose is so much more important and life-threatening than the fact that you are hot and stuck in a traffic jam. You see, ego will always require an answer, a 'Why?'

If you were in a place of soul, you would not react to this situation either way – you would just accept that these events were meant to occur exactly as they did. Now, don't get confused, this does not mean we let people walk all over us. What it does mean is that we address every situation from a place of understanding that there is a bigger picture. If we have issues with someone or something, we address them from a place of love. A place of wanting to understand the other person and most importantly, a place of listening. Remember we have two ears and one mouth for a reason.

At the end of the day, we are only human and it is not possible to continuously maintain this state. Part of our trials and tribulations as a human is not only to learn and grow and progress through this life, but also to awaken the soul within and experience a far more magnificent journey than one could ever imagine possible. It is truly in the 'ordinary' that an extraordinary life is possible, by recognising those moments.

In these ordinary moments, if we take on the possibility of learning and growing in a positive light as a chance to be all that we can be, then we will be far more conscious and alert in our daily lives. We will be more present in our interactions with people and the events that occur around us.

There are those truly blissful moments that reflect our humanity. When you are moved to tears by a certain event because you are deeply touched, this is because your true nature has been touched, and when that is touched, you can then connect with all others and their purposeful and true nature. You start to see things differently.

You start to see soul at work and you start to understand the really important things in life, like having connection, family, friends, love, laughter, community etc. I could go on and on.

You start to realise that everyone struggles with pain and has difficulties to overcome. You may not realise it yet, but we are all wounded somehow, some quite badly, others just slightly. But, what can we learn about these wounds that we carry?

The deep wound of losing my mum at such a young age has meant that I spend as much time with my son as I can. If I had not been given this gift, given this experience, I may have a child that I hardly do anything with and do not spend quality time with, because I don't have a compass that says 'this is important'. So, for that I am truly grateful.

Other people may spend lots of money on their children because they were once poor; or because they simply want their child to have the best. Where do you come from when you are parenting? What is important to you?

Then we can start to study pleasure and the need or desire we have to have pleasure in our life. What do you think is more motivating, pleasure or pain? You will be more motivated to move away from pain than towards pleasure every time. Why do you think that when you are thrown off a horse, the golden rule is you must get back on your trusty steed right away? If you don't, you are more likely to never get back on, as you will be afraid that it will happen again. You can see from this that you will be more motivated by pain.

While we all experience pleasure and pain in our lives differently, we also all experience both. We like pleasure in our lives and usually we run from pain.

You want your life to be spiritually guided, yet characteristically flavoured by ego, or your personality (the 'you' that you show to the world). People will see you moving physically as Tony or Rebecca etc. We do need an identity so that we can actually have interactions with each other. That is when the ego is born, when we name it and give it a powerful presence. After all, soul does not have a name, it does not need anything. Soul is soul however you look at it.

You are guided spiritually; after all, we are spiritual entities having an emotional experience in both a physical body and on a physical plane.

When you think about that, then you understand the spiritual, physical and emotional levels. There is nothing else. Take away that which animates us, our soul, or spirit, our very life force, and we are dead.

Does it matter then, the clothes we wore, the company we kept or the money we had? I don't think so. Then my question to you is, if it does not matter when you are dead, does it really matter when you are alive?

When you begin to move through your world on a soulful level, you begin to wish for others that they live in happiness and harmony, as you wish that for yourself. Your interactions with others then become a situation where this outcome is paramount in the way you live. This outcome will produce the greatest energetic vibration for all.

The most important thing here is to try to understand any situation from the other person's point of view. All agreements must have win/win outcomes. Nothing else is acceptable if you are living from a place of love, light and compassion.

I received a couple of emails that were quite scathing. I could have reacted to these emails with ego, or I could have done what I did and picked up the phone. I apologised, explained the place I was coming from and made an agreement to move forward with modified and conscious behaviour. EASY! My responses back from these people were so incredibly positive when I reached out with love, as opposed to reacting to the harshness in the emails.

There was no friction to grab on to once this occurred. There was simply a feeling of space and an end to the otherwise tumultuous behaviour. It simply evaporated; there was nothing for it to cling on to – nothing for it to perpetuate itself with.

It becomes easy, when you realise it is not all about you. When you take self out, you take the problem out. The counselling and Buddhist teachings I've received have helped me get to this understanding.

In another example, one of my friends was complaining that all she did was give to her friend. She was constantly giving food and lifts here and there. When she asked her friend Sam to buy her a coffee one day on the way to work, an altercation ensued. This was because there was no communication as to say why Sam should buy Denise a coffee. It was even stranger for the fact that Denise gave Sam so much. So here a small conversation would have helped them to understand their agreement and where they both came from.

You can never assume a situation. Everyone will move through their world from the only model they have, theirs. How often have I heard in practice, 'Everyone thinks like this, surely?' To which I always respond, 'No, pretty much only you'. It is a little like the fact that whatever car you drive, that is the one you see on the road all the time. You identify your world from your thoughts, values and beliefs and then assume that everyone else has these very same thoughts, values and beliefs! How egotistic! If every person in the world is different, no two people are alike, then surely their thoughts would be different too?

This is why you can never assume anything. You actually need to ask, you need to have a conversation and put your thoughts and ideas on the table. You do realise that there are more people in this world than just you, don't you?

So, in the situation of Denise and Sam, they could have a conversation that would go something like this: 'Sam, you know that I have been driving us both to work now for the last 6 months?' To which Sam would probably say, 'Yes'. To which Denise could respond, 'I was wondering if it is okay with you, if you buy the coffees on the way to work since then I would feel better about paying for the gas. Would this work for you?'

Do you see any friction here? It is honest and up-front. It deals with the issue, not the people involved, and it offers a solution to the problem. Do you have these conversations when issues arise, or does your conversation go something like: 'I am so sick of driving Sam to work, she really does not appreciate it and I have to always buy the gas'?

Which conversation do you resonate with? Which conversation would you like to resonate with?

The first conversation would alleviate any misunderstanding immediately. One of the most common mistakes is assuming you know what is going on. Never assume anything – ask someone. You operate from your model of the world and I operate from my model of the world, so our lives will be very different because our beliefs and values are very different.

I hope through this to be able to reach you on a level that really impacts your life deeply, and that you are able to move forward in your life from an even more enriched place of purpose and authenticity.

In this moment, I absolutely love what I am sharing. I am trying to help you see that it is the ordinary things which are so extraordinary to see and feel and experience. We are waiting for someone to show us the way, show us that we have arrived. The truth is, you arrived here spiritually the moment you were born. But you have been fighting with your true purpose and your true destiny, you have been letting ego run the ship, when in reality all you needed to do was turn the volume of your ego down and listen to your soul. All your answers are within, you just need to tune into them; turn them up, so to speak.

"When you are truly at your centre,
the madness of finding fault in others disappears."

Anonymous

- Chapter Thirty-Eight -
Personal Responsibility

"The price of greatness is responsibility."
Winston Churchill

When you want a situation to change, ask yourself, 'How have I contributed to this situation?' With your answer in mind, ask now, 'What do I need to change to help this situation?' That is taking personal responsibility. Rather than blaming or creating friction, you are looking for a solution inside yourself. Try it out for a week and see what happens.

Taking personal responsibility is taking charge of your life. It enables you to come from a place where change is possible. When you ask these questions, you are trying to understand the situation from a place of willingness to change, so you can effectively move forward. The only person that can change your life is you. If you use excuses, denial, justification, or blame, then this adds to the problem rather than helping you through it.

Not taking responsibility, using blame or excuses, gives your power away. This is like handing over the reins and expecting someone else to ride your horse while you are still sitting in the saddle. No wonder you don't end up where you want to go!

When I stayed in my relationship with Harry for so long after it stopped working for either of us, I did it because I did not want to take responsibility. I thought it would be easier to stay in the relationship, than to be strong and leave. My excuse was that I didn't want to hurt him, because he loved me. This way I could stay in the role I was playing as the victim, and not have to take responsibility for anything that I had created in my life.

Recognising and acknowledging your behaviour is the first step to changing it. Once you know what you are dealing with, you can take action to change and look for alternative ways of being.

It is tempting to avoid things which make us feel uncomfortable, so we can stay in our comfort zone. But it is only through stepping out of that comfort zone, that we can grow. When you come up against that place of discomfort, take a breath and move forward to expand yourself.

It takes at least three weeks to create a new habit. If you decide to manage situations differently, it will seem difficult at first, but the more you practise, the easier it will become.

- Chapter Thirty-Nine -
Letting Go

"Sometimes letting things go is an act of far greater power than defending or hanging on."

Eckhart Tolle - A New Earth

Imagine standing on the edge of the moment, letting go and having faith that the wind will allow you to glide effortlessly and safely. Knowing that following your dream is enough. At that moment, you release your ego to the wind and you evolve. Imagine the courage it takes for you to be comfortable doing this.

You are standing at the edge of a great sheer cliff. As you lean forward, moving your body weight from the ground to thin air, you are certain that you will surely die. It is a fact that you will most certainly perish and end up broken in a million pieces at the bottom of the cliff. Your mind is telling you to stop, telling you to keep your feet firmly on the ground. Your mind assures you that the life you have right now is awesome. Yet in your heart, you feel the need for more expansion – you want to know what possibilities exist for you. Deep within your soul, a tiny little voice cries out and if you are silent long enough you will hear it. The little, tiny voice says, 'Excuse me ... I think you can fly.'

Your mind knows this is ridiculous and is doing everything possible to keep you safe and away from that menacing edge. Your mind does not want to trust you, for it knows better. Your mind thinks it knows the answer to everything. Does it?

Stop for a minute and just imagine this possibility. What if, as you leaned forward, the wind effortlessly picked you up and floated you through the air on a journey you could never have even imagined, let alone had the joy to experience? What if this journey you were whisked away on, opened your heart and your eyes to a greater possibility and a greater understanding of life and happiness? What if this journey you were on was the greatest gift you had ever experienced and you didn't want to try because you are afraid? What do you need to let go of right now, in this very moment? Could it be fear of the unknown? Ooooooooh that's pretty scary!

Well, this is what I am alluding to when I talk about letting go. Let go of your perceptions of how you think it will all work out, because trust me, unless you are God, or some divine being like that, the way you think it will work out (your experience of life) and the actual way it WILL work out, will be worlds apart, I assure you.

So now, let go. Let go of your misconceptions, your preconceptions, and anything else you are holding onto.

Pick up your paintbrush and grab all the colours that you love. Your canvas is blank; what will you paint now that you know that anything is possible?

Letting go can be hard to do. Through our lives we have situations when we need to let go of ideas, beliefs, and sometimes we have to let go of people.

I have at times found some of the deepest pain when I have had to let go of something, especially of someone I love. I have had to deal with loss over and over again, and it is painful. Obviously this is the lesson that I need to master since it keeps showing up for me over and over.

If you had a severe injury, this would impact the way you functioned in the world mentally, physically, emotionally and perhaps spiritually. For example, if you had a burn on your arm and had a skin graft, then burnt your arm another seven times and had seven more skin grafts, that arm would perpetually be damaged, and quite deeply too. Probably after so many skin grafts, you would not have any sensation in your skin. It just may have been repaired too many times, which of course would mean that you were again more susceptible to a burn, because you would not be able to feel heat. Wow, what a huge hurdle. How do you overcome something like this? What would you need to heal and what would you need to learn?

This is similar to the way I feel loss. I have had to deal with loss so many times that the area inside my soul that deals with loss is completely traumatised. Yes, I have had all the counselling one would have time to have, or be able to pay for, yet this area is seriously wounded. So now, it's a matter of learning to let go, no matter what the consequences are, and understanding that there is a far greater picture to all of this than I may ever know. I can never assume that a situation that appears as 'letting go' will actually result in a similar pain. The truth is, I would not be able to project that sort of outcome, so why worry about something that has not yet happened?

Why is it that the person who is afraid of dogs will subconsciously bring the vicious dog closer to him/her? Whatever you put out there is what you draw to you. I would never bring a vicious dog close to me energetically. I am just not afraid of dogs and have not had any bad experiences with them.

In order to move forward and realise your potential, you must let go of thoughts and beliefs that are holding you back. What thoughts and beliefs do you have which are stopping you from living the greatest life ever? What thoughts and beliefs are holding you back from your true potential?

Once you have figured out what thoughts and beliefs are holding you back, you need to ask the more important question of how painful are these thoughts and beliefs? Remember, you will not fix what is not broken. You need to have a certain level of discomfort to make any change. Usually, the greater the degree of pain that you are in (mental, emotional, physical or spiritual) the greater the degree of necessity for you to actually take action.

My question to you is: how willing are you to change? How much pain are you living with? Is it enough to motivate you to change? In order for you to change, you will need to let go of something. Don't think of it as a loss though. If your glass of water is full to the brim, there is no space to add any more. If you tip some water out, you will create space to add something else. If you tip it all out, you could quite happily fill it up with an entirely different drink.

How much of what sort of life do you deserve? And when are you going to allow the possibility of change to occur? Is now too soon?

It's so easy to say that I will start this next week, or as a New Year's resolution, or whatever the case may be. In all honesty, when are you going to do it? If you truly honoured your life, you would start to do it NOW, in this very moment. So, my friend, what will it take for you to honour yourself? Let go of a few things to create the possibility of a few different things.

Start now, today. Make that change. Realise that each and every moment of your life is truly precious and reach in and honour that now!

If you were the only person ever in the history of the universe to have a life, this very life that you live now, you would not even experience 'good' or 'bad', you would be so busy trying to 'try life on'. You would be curious about how life fits, how it works, how you feel while you are living this so-called 'life'.

If you were the ONLY one to have a life, I would bet my last dollar that you would not be busy judging all the events and people around you. You would be soaking up the experience of life with amazement, in the way that young children do when they see or do something for the very first time. So, what will it take for you to begin to get excited about your life in this way? If you were the only person to have a life, to have the gift of life? I am sure that you would not be afraid to see what life could do, or bring you. You would not be afraid of consequences, seeing no one else had experienced this life. You would not be afraid to try and there would not be anyone telling you to 'be careful because ... '

You would step up and in and own it, grab it, and you would not let it go. You would hold onto it as if your very life depended on it. You would want to experience everything, good, bad and ugly, and probably at the end of it all you would say, 'That was one hell of a ride'.

If you are reading this book right now, you still have a chance to come from this place; you still have an opportunity to treasure this wondrous life. What are you waiting for?

Love it, live it, breathe it, lap it up, smother yourself in this thing called life. You have one shot at it – this is your only chance. Enjoy!

When we let go, when we are in a place of learning, often other issues such as grief, fear or anger, which are all ego by the way, will rise to the surface and shroud us in the states of emotion that they produce, e.g. sadness, anxiety, or rage. I find when I'm sad, I am grieving the loss of all losses of the past, I am grieving my disconnection from love, and this is not a comfortable place for me to come from.

Try writing a list of things that you feel are holding you back in life, that you want to get rid of. Perhaps it is negativity in your relationship with your partner or mother, the fact that you don't have enough money or enough education, or that you are too tall or too short. Once you have written your list, rip it up, or burn it. Say to yourself that you are letting go of these beliefs. Decide to leave them behind, and actively discard those thoughts if they try to creep back in. There will always be more to let go of, as you delve further into yourself and allow new possibilities in.

This constant letting go is a little like sweeping the kitchen floor. You can sweep the kitchen floor and it will be pristine, yet in a short time it will be dusty again. So you need to sweep regularly, to keep moving any negativity out of your life, and create a space for new possibilities to come in.

It's amazing how you can think that your life cannot possibly get better and then you can have an opportunity to experience something that can be so mind blowing and awesome. Yet, that is why life is such a gift. A while ago, I had the most magnificent day. I went sky diving.

Now, why would you need to go sky diving, you might ask? In the profession I work in, I help people get over their blocks. Whenever they are stuck emotionally or mentally, I have a wide variety of tools to help them transform their life.

One of the tools you may use for yourself is to notice where resistance shows up for you. Resistance is a place that you can find some of the greatest growth for yourself. If I feel any sort of resistance to anything, then I must move towards it. This is the place for the greatest learning for me, and often the greatest reward.

So, shall I go sky diving? These were my excuses: no, no, not me, I am a single mum with a young child. No, no, not me, I don't really need it. No, no, not me, after all, I have been on a screaming roller-coaster ride; one of those death-defying ones! Because I could feel this resistance inside, I woke up in the morning and said, 'I have to dive'.

It was the second most exhilarating day of my life, topped only by the birth of my child. The feeling of free fall is simply something that you can't explain. I understand that you only wear a parachute so that you can do it again. The rush I got from it, the sheer adrenaline, meant that I was up for thirty six hours straight! Even then, when I lay down, I was not sleepy. It was mind-blowing. Imagine if I had never done it, I would have missed this experience! I had to do it again, just to be sure – this time, I was diving head first – I was totally relaxed and at one with the world. I felt so spiritually connected and Zen; it was amazing. Now I want to do the course so I can dive by myself!

In that situation, when I had felt that sort of fear and resistance, what if I had just ignored it? What if I had simply gone on my merry way? I am so glad that I move towards my resistance and so should you; this is where your greatest gifts lie.

Most people don't do what I call 'critical thinking'. They never stop to think about their life, how it could be, or how it should be. They don't have a plan with a final desired destination for their life. They just keep doing the nine to five slog. Like a mouse on a treadmill, they simply keep going round and round. They expect a different outcome yet they don't do anything differently to get it! Now isn't that strange?

If you booked a ticket on a plane with no set destination, just a seat to go somewhere, where would you end up? Who knows? Well, this is how most people live their lives, blindly going with the flow wherever it takes them. How sad, that life should dictate their direction rather than their hopes and dreams and wishes directing their life. All you have to do is make a plan to get there. None of this is rocket science. When I am coaching my clients, I ask them how does their business 'end'. They look at me with that 'deer in the headlights' look. End? There is an end? Wow! I thought I was going to do this forever.

- Chapter Forty -
Goal Setting

"Those who do not create the future they want,
must endure the future they get."

Draper L. Kaufman, Jr

We each have a purpose in life; a journey to take that is completely unique to us. No two journeys are alike. No two people's lessons are alike. It is our individual nature and the way that we can learn and grow that has the most impact on the collective. In short, the most creative and flexible thinker will have the ability to produce dynamic results.

We each need to find our true path, our journey and our purpose. We each need to discover these things within ourselves, and each of our discoveries will be unique. Some people are born knowing what their path is and what they want to do or achieve in life. Others get a sense of it somewhere along the way. It is sad to say that some people go to their grave having never figured out their true purpose, or what they would like to achieve in their lifetime. Shame, such a shame.

When I was younger and full of joy, if I was around other people who were not joyous or happy, I would subdue my joy and happiness so as not to make anyone else feel bad. How tragic, that I would feel the need to snuff out my light so that someone else would not feel my joy. Where was the sense in that? In a misguided attempt to prevent others' pain, I just hurt myself. I did not want to inflict myself on anyone else.

Your only choice is to step forward, find your true purpose and shine. There is no huge neon sign that says 'You have made it'. What you do have are beautiful flowers, time with friends and family and redeemed social conditions – these are ordinary experiences that can create extraordinary outcomes and none of it is hard!

When I was living in the tent, I was completely dead inside and thought that I was about one hundred years old. I had given up on myself. How sad. I was totally worn out. I did not think there was a way out; I did not believe that I could change this. I had no concept that my life could be any better, let alone phenomenal. I was just going through the motions, completely empty and hollow inside.

I never thought I would get another bite of the cherry, so now two years down the track, to have the sort of life I have now is truly phenomenal. I feel so blessed. I have created it for myself! If I can create this, then what else can I create? The better I become at transforming my own life, the easier it is to jump the hurdles. As I master this, I can teach others how to jump also. Can you imagine a place where you say to yourself, 'Bring on the lessons; I can't wait to learn!'

We design and create our future around us exactly as we see it. We need to be very strategic about designing the life that we want to lead.

We need to live our lives 'on purpose'. If this is a new term to you, living on purpose is like living consciously, being awake and present in each moment. So many people are anaesthetized to their life and the potential that is open to them. So many people just go through the motions. This is not living – there is no 'living' in this.

Once you let go of all the rubbish and all the negativity, all the things that no longer serve you, then you will need a plan, a picture of your dream life. This is where a dream board or vision board can be useful. If you had a magic fairy wand and could create any life at all, how would that life look, what would you create?

I ask my clients to find a whole heap of magazines or pictures and start tearing the pictures out that resonate with them on a heart-felt level. This is so much fun that, before you know it, you have hundreds of great pictures in a heap on the floor.

Next, take a piece of cardboard and begin to design your dream life, by sticking on all the pictures that show how you would like to live. Under the pictures, I like to add statements and timeframes, such as 'I am now involved in the most amazing relationship of my entire life. I am happy and fulfilled and giddy with joy. All of this happens by ... and insert the date that you would wish it to occur by.

The client keeps their vision board on their desk to look at consciously and sub consciously each and every day. Then we build a plan for how they can achieve this. It is not enough to just create this vision; you need to take action as well. Just small steps to move you towards your goals. I love the analogy of training for a marathon.

If you were training for a marathon, you would not get up and run ten kilometres each day. That would just be silly, you would be so sore that you would never attempt it again. You would have a plan based on tiny bite sized steps, so that you could achieve your goal. On the first day of training, you would just put your runners on. Simple. As you can see, this step is so very tiny, that it would be embarrassing if you did not do it. So you have your runners on, and you are now officially in training. So easy! It was such a small step, hardly worth talking about. On day two, you would maybe run to the front door. Again, so easy and hardly worth talking about. On day three, you might decide to run out of the door. You get the picture – the steps that are required are each so small as to be hardly noticeable. However added together, they can achieve great things.

We way overestimate what we can do in the immediate future, yet we grossly underestimate what is possible five years out.

When you establish your vision and set tiny goals towards achieving it, you are more likely to be coming from a truly authentic and heartfelt space. You will be more likely to find that things flow easily to you.

So how do you recognise your own authenticity, your uniqueness if you like? If you are being and acting in an authentic manner, you would know that. It becomes obvious and clear, all your doors open to reveal this. There is no question about it; it is more of a certainty. You live your life from a heartfelt place; a place of love and light. You have a knowing that this is the truth that you walk; you are compelled to do it.

When you are in this 'heart' space, you don't care about the judgements of others, and instead wish them love and harmony in their life. You wish them a life free from suffering and you know you must take your own path because it is part of your destiny. For example, with my first retreat in Australia, I knew that I had to do it. There was no option – it was my destiny to make it happen no matter what. I made it happen and it was fantastic; people's lives were forever changed by it. I can't wait to do the next one. Again, it is my destiny to do them.

Every day I take a step forward, in the most authentic way that I can, and each step reveals a soul that is truly beautiful. A magical moment of being. Every day, I live from a space of love. I feel more and more connected to all living beings, animals too. We are the only species on the planet who have this capacity. How lucky are we to move forward in true faith and honesty. When the purpose is correct, then the path will reveal itself, when and how it is supposed to. The lesson of trust and faith can truly be a difficult one as it is not something tangible. You cannot physically touch or hold faith.

So then, what is faith and how important is it? The dictionary defines faith as, 'Confidence or loyalty to a person or thing, dogma or set of beliefs'. I think the key word here is 'confidence'. When you have confidence, or faith, in your beliefs and desires, then goal setting is easy, because in your heart you KNOW it must happen, because you have a strong faith that it will. Faith allows for the possibility of a new purpose, a new hope, a new dream. The new dream is as rain is to the dry earth. I step forward now, and all things around me flourish as my faith is unshakeable.

Most people are what I call the 'living dead'. They go

through the motions and don't ever stop to contemplate their actions. They would much rather stay with their flock than contemplate something that is different. Many people want to be accepted or liked and this will obviously colour the way they do things in the world. They curb their true natures in order to be accepted. How do you set goals and achieve amazing results if you are not prepared to one day fly?

These people are not living. They do not say, 'I am going to do this or that'. At the end of the day, the only person you can master is you! The only person you can change is also you. When you master yourself, you will master your life.

If you think more critically and strategically about your life, you will produce greater results. If you are asking yourself some of the following questions, then you are starting to think critically and strategically.

These questions help to align you on a soul, or spiritual, level. When you are not asking these questions, then you are quite often in ego.

I ask myself six questions each morning – three for quality of life and three for my business.

The three questions I ask myself about my quality of life are:

1) How can I be more love in each and every moment?

I ask myself this question because when I am in a state of wishing only the best for those around me, I am also in a state of flow. Energetically, I am open to greater possibility. This also means that I connect with all those that cross my path, on a heart level. What could be better than this? It means that I am conscious of trying to stay out of ego.

2) How can I be more grateful for the experiences in my life – whether they are good or bad? They are all just experiences at the end of the day.

This question allows me to open up to the possibility of abundance in my life; the possibility of living with extremely positive energy. Some of the great spiritual gurus in this world have said that being grateful is the most important quality to foster. If you have two arms and legs and are breathing, you probably have a great deal to be thankful for. You might not even be thinking about this until you lose something. As humans, we tend to have a need to compare ourselves and our situations to give us perspective and also to see how we fit in.

3) How can I serve more? How can I contribute more to other people?

Serving or contributing is one of the greatest gifts we can bestow on someone around us. I always like to come from a place of service. This means that I am aligned with soul and that my intent is for the greatest good of all. I like the humble feeling that I get when I am in a place of service. I absolutely love giving. I think many people benefit from giving. Who would you give to if you could?

On the business side of things, I ask myself the following questions:

1) How can my life become even more amazing each day?

I ask this because it prompts me to improve, to strive for even more fulfilment, happiness, freedom and joy.

To make sure I am always living an amazing life, I constantly look for possibilities and opportunities. If an opportunity comes into my life, I consider it, even if it seems to be outside what I would normally say yes to.

I like to think that if someone asked me if I could climb Mount Everest in a pair of sandals, I would at least try. Besides, with all that I have been through in my life, I think nothing is impossible. There are a few words that simply do not figure in my language. They are: bored, no and impossible.

I want to know what I am capable of in every fibre of my being. This is the true courage to live an ordinary life.

2) Is this the best use of my time right now?

Asking this question is critical. So many of us, myself included, get hooked up in procrastination, or doing things with no end result, or not even knowing why you are doing something, just doing it because you have always done it.

Let's think about this for a minute. Is just doing something because you have always done it, the best use of your time right now? I am going to say probably not. While it is not the best use of your time right now, your results will not be the best either. If you want to improve your life and get great results, you really need to analyse what you are doing with your time. After all, time is the only commodity that you cannot buy more of, so that makes it even more precious. One of the most powerful questions I ask myself and my clients in relation to time is, 'If you had seven days left to live, what would you do with your time?' All of a sudden, you start coming up with some very real answers, because suddenly you have seven days rather than the fifty years you thought you were going to live!

It is Sunday morning and I am writing while my son lies downstairs watching TV. He has whooping cough. Is this the best use of my time right now? Absolutely. If my son was well, I would be playing with him. He needs some quiet time so I am using my time to be productive. I am writing because I have a plan, a dream and a vision for my life. Before I die, I want to help a million people. So if I think I can, then I want to try. So I have checked, and yes, this is the best use of my time.

3) How can I leverage my business and do more with less?

This used to be the hardest question for me to fully understand, because I simply did not get the concept of leverage. I did not understand the mentality of doing more with less. I did not understand that you could leverage both your business and your life to even greater heights. In terms of living an amazing life, when you figure the leverage part out, your life will become something truly extraordinary.

I want to produce bigger and better results with less effort and in less time. This part of my life is kind of like a game – how can I make the greatest play with the most minimal effort? I have fun with this.

Leverage often comes in the form of a team, systems, or a greater opportunity. I hold retreats around the world to help people get over their blockages. I am able to help people transform their lives as I have transformed my life.

You need structure in place and discipline to create freedom. You need goals to work towards to stretch yourself, and you need to contribute in this world. So what are you waiting for?

You must be clear about the vision and goals you have for your life and then you take tiny steps towards those goals. You need to work towards these goals, a little bit each week, in a set timeframe. You need the desire to achieve these goals, the discipline to do the work required and a big WHY, which will be your motivating force. For me, my why came in a very small package, my son. He was, and still is, my reason for achieving the goals I achieve today. My son was going to have swim lessons and he was not going to eat another lentil in his life if I could help it.

When you start to master these skills, then you can step into a bigger arena and realise that you can do so much more. Create even more worthwhile goals. How would you feel then?

The whole point of this is so that you can live an amazing life. You want to be aligned with your soul. Your sense of self-fulfilment will be so much greater. You will be at peace. Content within.

- Chapter Forty-One -
Gratitude And Abundance

"The universe loves grateful people.
The more you are grateful for, the more you get to be
grateful about. It's that simple. We like to complicate
things a lot, but we don't have to."

Louise Hay

Recognising the extraordinary in our ordinary lives is a state of bliss that anyone can achieve. When you are grateful for what you have, you are positively acknowledging a benefit you have or will receive. This attracts more for you to be grateful for in your life.

The losses I've had in my life have contributed to my ability to be grateful for what I have and experience now. I have learned to be grateful for the small as well as the large experiences, because I have drawn them to me and am responsible for them. I accept my life as it is, because it is the masterpiece that I am creating from a blank canvas. Only I hold the paintbrush and only I choose the colours.

I am often asked how to create abundance. When I lived through a long period of poverty and scarcity, I was in a victim mentality. When I was homeless and going to the food bank for food, I was rarely asked out to dinner. I was rarely offered help. There was no money flowing my way because I was in a state of contraction. I was shrinking away from life, money and everything I was afraid of. I was constantly struggling, wanting more, and feeling that I was so unlucky. I kept asking for more but nothing came to me.

Once I understood how this was creating my reality, I was able to turn it around. I concentrated on being grateful for the small things that I did have. I acknowledged and appreciated the abundance around me. This allowed a space where more could come into my life. When a little more trickled in I was grateful for that, and so a little more was able to come. On and on this cycle went, until I had created the flood of abundance that now surrounds me.

> *"Not what we have, but what we enjoy,*
> *constitutes our abundance."*
>
> John Petit-Senn

Only recently, I was reminded of just how much has changed, how much abundance I now allow into my life. I was at the airport with my son, and at the check-in counter I was given two $50 vouchers for meals. The vouchers were stamped 'for late check-in'. I pointed out to the man that we had lots of time and he replied with a wink, 'Just take it, it's on me'. I said, 'Thank you, I am very grateful'.

With the vouchers we bought a Japanese meal in the food hall, and started looking for somewhere to sit. There was not a seat to be found. Suddenly, a man stood up, midway through his meal, and offered us his table. I declined as he hadn't even finished eating. He insisted, because I had a child with me. In the space of a few minutes I had manifested a meal and a table. When we got on the plane, the man who had given his seat to us in the food hall was seated next to us on the plane. I do not believe in coincidences.

After we took off, the hostess moved through the plane, offering food and drinks for purchase. She stopped to chat with my son, and admire the colouring he was doing in his book. For no reason she said, 'You are my favourite guys on the plane, and your meals are on me.' I thanked her very much.

These may have been just free meals and convenient seating, but they were examples of the small abundances that are always at work, if we choose to see them and be grateful for them.

"Abundance is not something we acquire.
It is something we tune into."
Dr Wayne W. Dyer

Buddhist monks spend a lot of time in silence and stillness, appreciating the small moments in life. They understand the power of these moments, and fill them with gratitude, love and compassion. I try to learn from their example.

People who live from a space of abundance, simply create more abundance, whatever that is for them – money, love, physical or spiritual contentedness.

"Whatever we are waiting for - peace of mind,
contentment, grace, the inner awareness of simple
abundance - it will surely come to us, but only when we
are ready to receive it with an open and grateful heart."
Sarah Ban Breathnach

I was at a Neuro-Linguistic Programming training session when I realised how much my mindset had changed around abundance. Like many courses, there was a point where participants were offered the opportunity to attend further courses at a higher level of learning. The sales lady was telling me how my income would increase dramatically if I attended the next course. Without thinking, I turned to her and said, 'I am the fountain of wealth'. What a thing to say! What a thing to think! A fountain, a never ending stream of wealth. That was the message that came out of my mouth without thinking. I truly believed it, after all these years I was no longer in my poverty mentality, I was finally rich on the inside as well as the outside.

To tune in to abundance, practise recognising it when you see it. Rather than wishing you had more of something, look around you and notice what is already there in abundance. It could be physical or emotional. You may be surrounded by an abundance of cars, people, books, flowers, plants, pens, paper, wood on the floor, blinds on the window, dots on your shirt or spots on your skin. Once you start to take notice of it you will see that you are surrounded by an abundance of abundance.

Don't get caught up in judging whether the abundance is 'good' or 'bad'. It just is. For instance, you might have an abundance of dirty dishes in the sink. It doesn't matter if you would prefer not to have all those dishes, they are there, and they are abundant.

- Chapter Forty-Two -
Moving Forward

"You only keep what you give away."
RE Phillips

From the depths of my heart, I wish for you all, happiness, freedom, peace, harmony and abundance. I wish for you to realise your truest and fullest potential.

Every thought we have becomes part of the collective consciousness of the planet. Knowing that your thoughts contribute to the collective consciousness, ask yourself: what thoughts are you putting out there? When we use our energy to vibrate from our greatest purpose and the greatest good for all, we emanate light to all beings. This light can dispel other's darkness, uncertainty and fears.

By being in a state of love and light, you open the door of possibility and awareness for those who are unaware and possibly consumed by negative states, such as grief, fear and greed. You offer them a chance for transformation purely by your being.

Living from a place of kindness, love and peace creates more kindness, love and peace in this world. Your life is a reflection of your thoughts and actions.

You may be trying to attract what you desire, yet you cannot sit and wait for all these great things to come to you. You must build a plan with small and achievable steps that are time-framed and easily achievable.

We have an opportunity to experience a greater sense of oneness with ourselves, all others and the universe in general. When we come from a place of love, and we are centred and grounded in this space, we can appreciate it and be aware of it as our only way to live.

We begin to realise that each and every day is a blessing.

Miracles occur in our lives every day, we just need the awareness to see these 'miracles'. There are so many things we can be grateful for at any moment in time.

When we are in this space of gratitude, we bring goodness closer to ourselves and this then triggers even more goodness for ourselves and others. We increase the opportunity for connection among all living beings.

By being grateful, you realise how beautiful your friendships are, how delightful a brightly coloured bunch of gerberas is. You see the warmth in the smile of a child and you start to see the world through wondrous eyes again as you did when you were a child, innocent and pure.

You see that life's lessons create amazing opportunities to learn and grow, and you appreciate these lessons which you are blessed to receive. When we are grateful we are happy and see our days filled with happiness and joy, no matter what is going on.

When we are grateful, we are more likely to share. We are continuously showered with gifts from the universe and the more we appreciate this, the more abundant these gifts become. When we are grateful, we create a communion between the spiritual and the physical world in which we live.

Allow love to flow into your life and the lives of others. Remember to be grateful each and every day for all the amazing things in your life. We are the embodiment of our future for the planet, so create amazing dreams and begin to fulfil them. Then we can see what kind of a world it is possible to live in. The ripple effect will be astonishing when you come from a place of love and light. Shine, as brightly as you can. It is your duty to yourself and to everyone else.

Recommended Reading

You Can Heal Yourself   - Louise Hay
You Can Heal Yourself: The Movie   - Louise Hay
Long Walk To Freedom   - Nelson Mandela
Albert Schweitzer: A Biography   - James Brabazon
Mother Teresa: A Complete Authorized Biography
                                                    - Kathryn Spink
The Tibetan Book of Living and Dying   - Sogyal Rinpoche
The Road Less Travelled   - M Scott Peck
The Power of Now   - Eckhart Tolle
A New Earth   - Eckhart Tolle
Emptiness Dancing   - Adyashanti
God on A Harley   - Joan Brady
The Four Agreements   - Don Miguel Ruiz
Mutant Message Down Under   - Marlo Morgan
The Alchemist   - Paulo Coelho
A Fine Balance   - Rohinton Mistry
Angela's Ashes   - Frank McCourt
The Fountainhead   - Ayn Rand
Think and Grow Rich   - Napoleon Hill
Awaken the Giant Within   - Tony Robbins
Chicken Soup For The Soul   - Jack Canfield

Namaste

Coming Soon From Rhiannon Rees

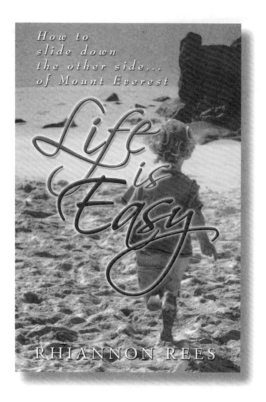

My next book, *Life Is Easy*, is the sequel to *How To Climb Mount Everest in Sandals*.

This book will focus in more detail on HOW TO create an extraordinary life.

It will break down and workshop the point-by-point issues you need to consider and think about critically, so you can make your life unfold as you desire.

It will contain step-by-step instructions on how to build a plan to develop your life and business into a masterpiece.

There will be a series of interviews and case studies from my coaching practice, to give examples of HOW this works.

For further details, please visit www.LoveLivingThe Dream.com

Spend Some Time With Rhiannon

'Journey To The Inner You' retreats

Presented by

LOVE
LIVING THE
DREAM

MAGIC MUMS CHARITY

Take a look at the 'Rhiannon gives back' program where single mums have the opportunity to be coached by Rhiannon to change their lives and reach their full potential – this FREE program is by application only – see www.LoveLivingTheDream.com for details

---

Attending one of my personal development retreats is the ultimate way to immerse yourself in the teachings introduced in this book.

In 1995, I conducted my first retreat, the only retreat I intended to do. The amazing developments the participants achieved created a demand for more retreats, and I've been conducting them ever since. I love watching people light up and grow, right in front of me!

There are two or three retreats each year. We started in North America, and in 2010, expanded to Australia, with other countries now also interested.

The retreats run for four or five days and offer the chance to immerse yourself in tools and disciplines to help you to get the most out of your life, and live a life of empowerment.

We have talks by guest speakers, such as Emma Sutherland, natural health practitioner from the TV show: *Eat Yourself Sexy*, speaking on health and nutrition; Amelia Burton, health and fitness coach, health and fitness expert from Australia's *Kerri Ann Show*, gives talks on exercise and health; Rod Lee, the Dalai Lama's bodyguard of fifteen years, teaches meditation and tai chi; and I give talks on various topics, such as critical thinking, true responsibility, team building, creating your future and more.

There are also psychology sessions around clearing your personal barriers, building a plan to change your life, creating dream boards and developing communication with yourself and others so you can move forward.

We also like to have a lot of fun!

We keep the numbers small to ensure there is an individual focus. The intimate team is empowering in itself, as you get the multi-powered dynamics of growth, encouragement and empowerment amongst you, as the days unfold.

The retreats provide a fun and supportive environment, where the focus is on learning, growing and taking steps forward.

Here is what some people had to say about their *Love Living The Dream* retreat experience:

'I could never have imagined what this course was going to be. I feel more at ease with myself. I have direction and purpose. I am much happier with myself. I truly believe everyone should have the opportunity to experience this course.'
- Brett

'This amazing course teaches you to love and honour yourself. To hear your inner voice and soul. To laugh at yourself and to "let go" of your baggage through the shedding of skin. Focus on you and become more of a whole person. Amazing – thank you.'
- Julie

'I was drawn to this class. I am so glad that I went with it. It was a fabulous experience. I think this is the beginning of an ongoing process, if I weren't a part of this group I'd probably be some dental assistant, bored, unfulfilled and constantly wondering if there was something else I could have in my life. This course has opened me up immensely. It has steered me to myself. Towards what I truly want, love and need in my life. It was fun too! Rhiannon, you are such a humble, humorous and great teacher – this is both special and a rarity. Thank you.'
- Holly

'Thank you for all your help. I am now so much more aware of my inner self. I now know how to achieve peace and tranquillity. I have learned to accept my past hurts and continue to live through and past it. You are a wonderful, warm, loving and caring teacher Rhiannon. Thank you. I now see life differently. I see sunshine where there were only clouds.'
- Susan

There are only fifty tickets to each retreat. Do yourself a favour and be one of those ticket holders so that you can live the life you deserve. More information is at: www.LoveLivingTheDream.com

An extraordinary life, gems of wisdom, and inspiration in a first release book by one of the world's best self development experts

Rhiannon Rees is referred to as Australia's answer to US self-help guru, Dr Wayne W Dyer.

She has worked with stars including the Spice Girls, X-Files and Grey's Anatomy, and was awarded 4th best business coach in the world in 2010. After overcoming huge adversity and achieving a substantial education and success, she continues to inspire people around the world to live their lives to the fullest, in her first book, *How To Climb Mount Everest in Sandals.*

Rhiannon puts her extensive experience and qual-ifications as a humanitarian, business coach, homeopath, entrepreneur, presenter, mother of one and lover of life into this extraordinary book.

Rhiannon Rees is renowned in her field of self development. She has featured in countless TV and radio shows and in print publications in both Australia and North America, recounting her own life as a homeless single mother, and sharing the steps she made to becoming a specialist in her field, helping others to live the life of their dreams. Rhiannon Rees' life mission, including writing this book, (the runner up in the New South Wales 'Franchise Woman of the Year Australia 2010' and a nominee for 'Telstra Business Woman of the Year 2010'), is to assist and empower as many people as possible to live full lives of happiness, meaning, fun, and passion.

This first release book, *How To Climb Mount Everest in Sandals*, highlights the raw, courageous and heart wrenching story of Rhiannon's life that will set sparks flying inside readers and inspire many to live the life of their dreams. It can make the seemingly impossible things seem possible, like climbing Mount Everest in sandals. After losing everything, Rhiannon learns how to embrace the ordinary moments in life, and realises how very extraordinary they can be, and she inspires the reader to do the same.

Rees commented: *'I lost my innocence through child sexual abuse, lost contact with my mother for most of my childhood, lost my brother to suicide, lost five babies to miscarriage, lost all my money, lost my husband to his other identity as a woman, and even lost the roof over my head and became homeless. Each of these losses carved into my soul, and I thought I would never survive. But I did.'*

'I spent years in analysis, immersing myself in self knowledge, to advance myself spiritually and gain insight into getting the most out of life. But it seemed that all the books I read focused on achieving the peaks,

getting to the top of the mountain ahead of everyone else. No one talked about just being. What about the simple satisfaction of being born, going to school, having a job, getting married, having kids and growing old? Being happy and content just living an ordinary life? Perhaps achieving these seemingly small goals was not as ordinary as I had first thought. Perhaps what I had thought was ordinary, was actually extraordinary?'

'Being able to inspire and help people to live their best life (in whatever area that is for them) through my retreats, speaking through the media, and with my coaching is for me, living the life of my dreams.'

How To Climb Mount Everest in Sandals is available in all good book stores in Australia and New Zealand, and via: *www.LoveLivingTheDream.com*

Rhiannon is available to talk about the book and any other topics to help people jump over their hurdles, including business, personal development, goal setting, overcoming obstacles, creating success and wealth, relationships, love, harmony, health, homeopathy, happiness, alternative medicine, team work, human resources and more.

I love you.